COGAT®

GRADE 2

VERBAL

3 Practice Tests
Level 8

Savant Test Prep™

www.SavantPrep.com

Please leave a review for this book!

Thank you for purchasing this resource.

Please take a moment to leave a
review on the website where you purchased this.

TABLE OF CONTENTS

INTRODUCTION

COGAT® GENERAL INFORMATION

- COGAT® stands for Cognitive Abilities Test®.
- The test measures students' reasoning skills and problem-solving skills.
- It provides educators with an overall assessment of students' academic strengths and weaknesses.
- The COGAT® is commonly used as a screener for gifted and talented programs.
  - Gifted and Talented (G&T) selection sometimes requires a teacher recommendation as well.
- The test is usually administered in a group setting.
- A teacher (or other school associate) administers the test, reading the directions.
- Please check with your school/testing site regarding its testing procedures, as these may differ.

COGAT® LEVEL 8 FORMAT

- Students in second grade take the COGAT® Level 8.
- The Verbal Battery has 54 questions.
- The test is divided into 3 main parts, each called a "Battery." Each Battery has three question types. See the chart below.

VERBAL BATTERY	NON-VERBAL BATTERY	QUANTITATIVE BATTERY
Picture Analogies: 18 Questions	Figure Analogies: 18 Questions	Number Puzzles: 14 Questions
Picture Classification: 18 Questions	Figure Classification: 18 Questions	Number Series: 18 Questions
Sentence Completion: 18 Questions	Paper Folding: 14 Questions	Number Analogies: 18 Questions

- Often, schools administer one Battery per day, allowing approximately 45 minutes per Battery.
- Students have around 15 minutes to complete each question type (for example, students would have around 15 minutes to complete Picture Analogies).
- See the following pages for examples and explanations of each question type.

COGAT® SCORING

- Students receive points for correct answers. Points are not deducted for incorrect answers. (Therefore, students should at least guess versus leaving a question blank.)
- In general, schools have a "cut-off" COGAT® score, which they consider together with additional criteria, for gifted & talented acceptance. This varies by school.
- This score is usually at least 98%. (However, some schools accept scores of 95% or even 85%.)
- A score of 98% means that your child scored as well as, or better than, 98% of those in his/her testing group.
- COGAT® scores are available for the entire test and can be broken down by Battery.
- Depending on the school/program, such a "cut-off" score may only be required on one or two of the Batteries (and not on the test overall).
- It is essential to check with your school/program for their acceptance procedures.
- The COGAT® Practice Tests in this book can not yield these percentiles because they have not been given to a large enough group of students to produce an accurate comparison/calculation.

HOW TO USE THIS BOOK

1. Go over the Question Examples together with your child. These begin on the next page.

2. Do Practice Test 1 (Workbook Format)
- Do these questions with your child, especially if this is your child's first exposure to COGAT®-prep questions. These questions have a "workbook format," meaning they are meant to be done together.
- Do not assign a time limit.
- Talk about what the question is asking your child to do.
- Questions progress in difficulty. (The first few questions are quite simple.)
- Go over the answers using the Answer Key.
- For questions missed, go over the answers again, discussing what makes the correct answer better than the other choices.

3. Do the remaining Practice Tests following Practice Test 1.
- If your child progressed easily through Practice Test 1, see how well they can do without your help.
- If your child needed assistance with much of Practice Test 1, then continue to assist your child with Practice Test 2.
- If you wish to assign a time limit, assign around 15 minutes per question type.
- Go over the answers using the Answer Key.
- For questions missed, go over the answers again, discussing what makes the correct answer better than the other choices.

4. Need more practice?

- **Help your child ace the test!**

- **Check out Savant Test Prep™ books on Amazon®.**

TEST-TAKING TIPS

- Ensure your child listens carefully to the directions, especially in the Sentence Completion section.
- Make sure (s)he does not rush through questions. (There is no prize for finishing first!) Tell your child to look carefully at the question. Then, tell your child to look at each answer choice before marking his/her answer.
  - If you notice your child continuing to rush through the questions, tell him/her to point to each part of the question. Then, point to each answer choice.
- If (s)he does not know the answer, then use the process of elimination. Cross out any answer choices which are clearly incorrect, then choose from those remaining.
- This tip/suggestion is entirely at your discretion. You may wish to offer some sort of special motivation to encourage your child to do his/her best. An extra incentive of, for example, an art set, a building block set, or a special outing can go a long way in motivating young learners!
- The night before testing, make sure your child has enough sleep, without any interruptions. (Think about the difference in **your** brain function with a good night's sleep vs. without. The same goes for your child's.)
- The morning before the test, ensure your child eats a healthy breakfast with protein and complex carbs. Do not let them eat sugar, chocolate, etc.
- If you can choose the time your child will take the test (for example, if (s)he will take the test individually, instead of at school with a group), opt for a morning testing session, when your child will be most alert.

QUESTION EXAMPLES

- Here is an overview of the COGAT® question types.
- This section has <u>simple</u> examples, to introduce your child to test concepts.
    - Do these examples together with your child.
- Below the questions are explanations for parents.

1. PICTURE ANALOGIES (VERBAL BATTERY)

• **Directions (read to child):** The pictures in the top boxes go together in some way. Look at the bottom boxes. One box is empty. Look at the row of pictures next to the boxes. These are the answer choices. Which one of these choices goes with the picture in the bottom box like the pictures in the top boxes go together?

• **Explanation (for parents):** Your child must figure out how the images in the top set of boxes are related and belong together. Then, (s)he must figure out which answer choice would go with the bottom left image so that the bottom set would have the same analogous relationship as the top set. (The small arrows demonstrate that the images go together.)

• **Strategy 1:** Define a "rule" to describe how the top set belongs together. Then, take this "rule" and use it with the bottom picture. Look at the answer choices, and figure out which answer would make the bottom set follow your "rule."

• **Using the above question as an example, say to your child:**
In this question, we see a spider and a web. A spider's home is its web. A rule would be, "the thing in the first box has as its home the thing in the second box." On the bottom, we see a bird. Let's try the answer choices with our rule. A flower is not correct because a bird's home is not a flower, nor is a bench or another bird. A nest is correct because it's a bird's home.

• **Strategy 2:** Try to come up with a sentence to describe how the top set belongs together. Then, use this sentence with the bottom picture. Look at the answer choices, and figure out which answer would make the sentence work with this bottom set. With both strategies, if more than one answer choice works, then you need a more specific rule/sentence.

• The examples on the next page outline some of the logic used in analogy questions. While the COGAT® uses pictures (not words) at this level in verbal analogies, this will still help familiarize your child with analogy logic.

• Directions (read to child): I am going to read you a question. The words go together in some way. One word is missing. Next, I will read you the answer choices. Let's figure out which one is the missing word.
(Parent note: the answer and logic are below the question.)

Question	Answer Choices			
1. Spider -is to- Web as Bird -is to- ? *Answer - Nest (Animal: Animal's Home)*	Flower	Bench	Nest	Bird
2. Acorns -are to- Squirrel as Seeds -are to- ? *Answer - Bird (Animal: Animal's Food)*	Grass	Bird	Fish	Snake
3. Calf -is to- Cow as Cub -is to- ? *Answer - Tiger (Animal Baby: Animal Adult)*	Tiger	Horse	Goose	Bull
4. Lion -is to- Fur as Snake -is to- ? *Answer - Scales (Animal: Animal's Covering)*	Lizard	Hair	Fangs	Scales
5. Happy -is to- Sad as Wet -is to- ? *Answer - Dry (Opposites)*	Damp	Clean	Water	Dry
6. Tiger -is to- Cheetah as Butterfly -is to- ? *Answer - Moth (Similar: Similar (Flying Insects))*	Bird	Bat	Moth	Jaguar
7. Flower -is to- Bouquet as Kernel -is to- ? *Answer - Corn Cob (Part: Whole)*	Snack	Plant	Corn Cob	Crop
8. Ship -is to- Port as Car -is to- ? *Answer - Garage (Object: Location)*	Truck	Garage	Marina	Wheel
9. Pencil -is to- Paper as Paint -is to- ? *Answer - Wall (Object: Object Used With)*	Wall	Color	Red	Light
10. Lumber -is to- Fence as Paper -is to- ? *Answer - Book (Object: Product That Object Is Put Together To Make)*	Log	Branch	Tree	Book
11. Cheese -is to- Refrigerator as Ice -is to- ? *Answer - Freezer (Object: Item Used to Store/Hold Object)*	Snow	Toaster	Freezer	Cube
12. Box -is to- Cube as Globe -is to- ? *Answer - Sphere (Object: Similar Shape)*	Prism	Sphere	Oval	Pentagon
13. Straw -is to- Juice as Spoon -is to- ? *Answer - Cereal (Utensil: Object Utensil Is Used With)*	Cereal	Salad	Steak	Sandwich
14. Egg -is to- Chicken as Milk -is to- ? *Answer - Cow (Food/Drink: Source of Food/Drink)*	Chick	Cheese	Rooster	Cow
15. Ambulance -is to- Paramedic as Tractor -is to- ? *Answer - Farmer (Vehicle: User)*	Doctor	Teacher	Scientist	Farmer
16. Doctor -is to- Stethoscope as Carpenter -is to- ? *Answer - Hammer (Worker Who Uses Object: Object)*	Boot	Builder	Cabinet	Hammer

2. PICTURE CLASSIFICATION (VERBAL BATTERY)

• **Directions (read to child):** The top row shows three pictures that are alike in some way. Look at the bottom row. There are four pictures. Which picture in the bottom row goes best with the pictures in the top row?

• **Explanation (for parents):** Together with your child, try to figure out a "rule" describing how the top pictures are alike and belong together. Then, apply the "rule" to each answer choice to determine which one follows it. If your child finds that more than one choice follows the rule, then a more specific rule is needed.

• **Using the above question as an example, say to your child:** In the top row, we see a ladybug, a party hat, and a dog. What do these have in common? It may be hard to see at first. Let's have another look. Each of these has spots. This is how they are alike. The only answer choice that has spots is the cheetah.

• **Tip:** You can help your child improve classification using items you see in everyday life or in books.

• The classification examples on the next page outline some of the logic used in classification questions. While the COGAT® uses pictures (not words) at this level in verbal analogies, this will still help familiarize your child with classification logic.

• Directions (read to child): I am going to read you a group of words. The words go together in some way. Let's figure out how the words go together. Then, I will read you another group of words. Let's figure out which one from this group goes best with the words in the first group.

(Parent note: the answer and logic are below the question.)

Question					Answer Choices			

1. Cave   Hive   Web | Spider   Nest   Vet   Bat
Answer - Nest (Animal Homes)

2. Butterfly   Ant   Bee | Worm   Horse   Bird   Dragonfly
Answer - Dragonfly (Animal Types (Insects)

3. Forest   Jungle   Desert | Tree   Valley   Rainforest   City
Answer - Rainforest (Habitats)

4. Lemon   Grape   Apple | Strawberry   Farm   Sweet   Lettuce
Answer - Strawberry (Kinds of Food (Fruit))

5. Scientist   Nurse   Detective | Superhero   Teenager   Pilot   Fairy
Answer - Pilot (Jobs)

6. Sock   Skate   Boot | Slipper   Cap   Mitten   Toe
Answer - Slipper (Objects Worn On Feet)

7. Hot Air Balloon   Jet   Helicopter | Ship   Airport   Bird   Airplane
Answer - Airplane (Vehicles for Air Travel)

8. Ruler   Measuring Tape   Scale | Thermometer   TV   Pen   Number
Answer - Thermometer (Object Use (Used to Measure)

9. Pillow   Blanket   Mattress | Towel   Chair   Sheet   Table
Answer - Sheet (Object Location (Found on Beds))

10. Fire   Sun   Stove | Cookie   Toaster   Beach   Camp
Answer - Toaster (Object Characteristics (Provide Heat))

11. Planet   Ball   Globe | Country   Goal   Bubble   Racetrack
Answer - Bubble (Object Shape (Spherical))

3. SENTENCE COMPLETION (VERBAL BATTERY)

• **Directions (read to child):** Listen to the question, then choose the best answer.

Which one of these shows a pair?

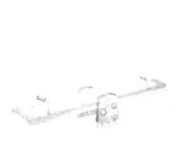   

• **Explanation (for parents):** Unlike Picture Analogies and Picture Classification, Sentence Completion questions have different directions. The above example is a very simple one. (The answer is C.) The questions in this book's two practice tests will be more challenging.

• Make sure your child listens carefully to these questions. Test administrators will not repeat the questions.

• If listening is challenging for your child, tell him/her to repeat the directions back to you. Remind your child to listen to the entire question. (Some children will stop listening if they think they already know the answer.)

• Tell him/her to pay special attention to "negative" words like "not" or "no." (The two practice tests include questions like this.)

Practice Test 1 (Workbook Format) begins on the next page.

Parents, read the below with your child.

Watch out!

This book is filled with tricky questions. Can you answer them?

 Of course you can!

Pay close attention to each question and try your best.

We'll be here to help you along the way!

COGAT® PRACTICE TEST 1
(WORKBOOK FORMAT)

PICTURE ANALOGIES

What goes in the empty box?

Sara

Directions (read to child): The pictures in the top boxes go together in some way. One box on the bottom is empty. Look at the row of pictures next to the boxes. These are the answer choices. Which one of these goes with the picture in the bottom box like the pictures in the top boxes go together?

Explanation (for parents): A more detailed explanation and example questions are on p. 6-7. If you have not already, look these over. Following is an excerpt.

Your child must figure out how the images in the top set of boxes are related and belong together. Then, (s)he must figure out which answer choice would go with the bottom left image so that the bottom set would have the same analogous relationship as the top set. (The small arrows demonstrate that the images go together.)

Example (read this to child): Look at the boxes on top. In the first box, we see a saw. In the second box, we see a tree. (Together, try to come up with a "rule" describing how they are alike and go together.) A saw is used to cut a tree. Let's look in the bottom box. We see a kitchen knife . Now, let's look at the answer choices. Which one goes with the picture of a knife in the same way that the pictures in the top row go together? The apple (the third choice). A kitchen knife is used to cut an apple.

Parent note: A common mistake for kids would be picking an answer that simply "has to do with" the first box. There is more than one answer choice that "has to do with" a kitchen knife. A fork has to do with a knife, since they are both utensils. However, a fork does not follow the rule, and it does not have the same relationship. Also, watch out for answer choices that have to do with objects on the top row. For example, a wrench has to do with a saw (both are tools). A forest has to do with a tree. However, neither of these follows the rule.

1.

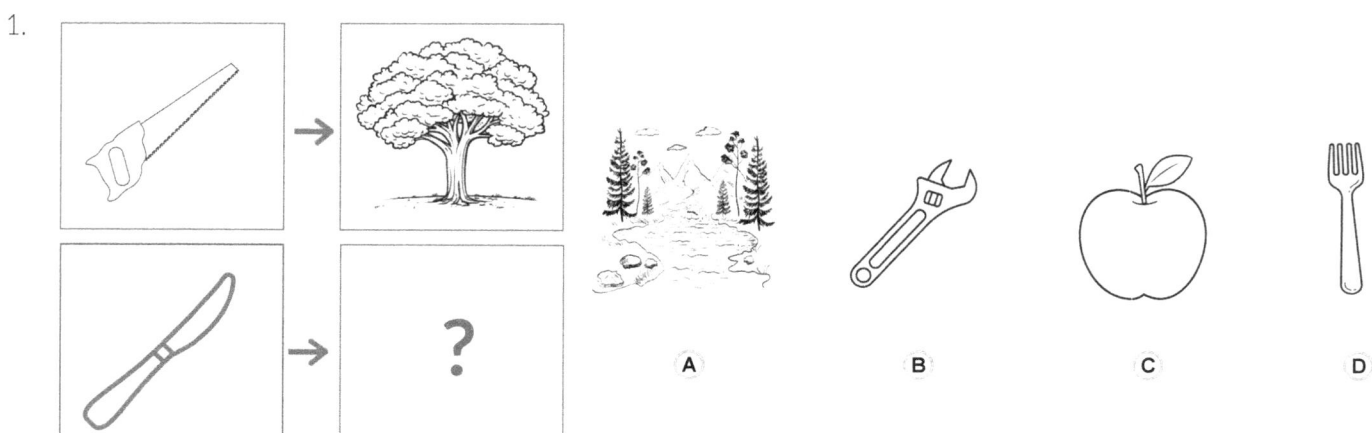

A   B   C   D

2.

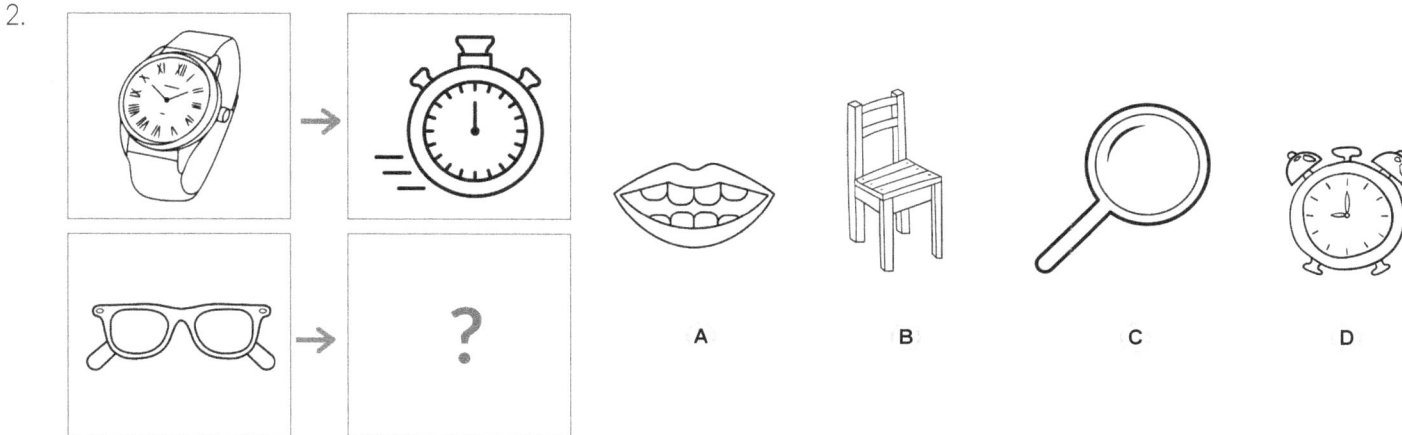

A   B   C   D

3.

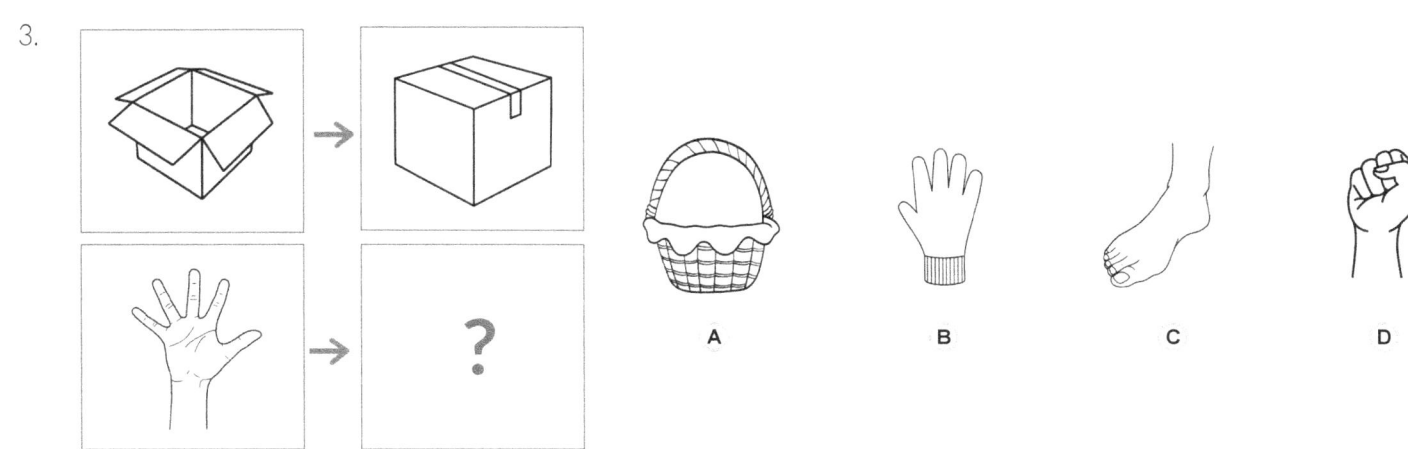

A   B   C   D

4.

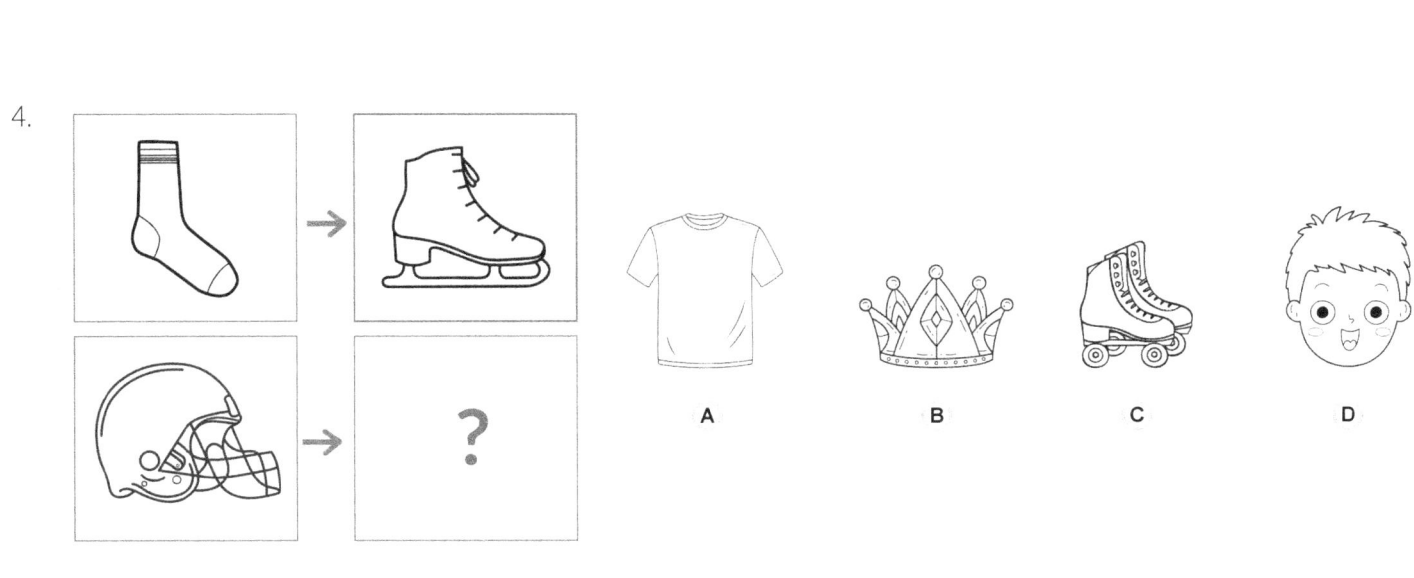

A   B   C   D

5.

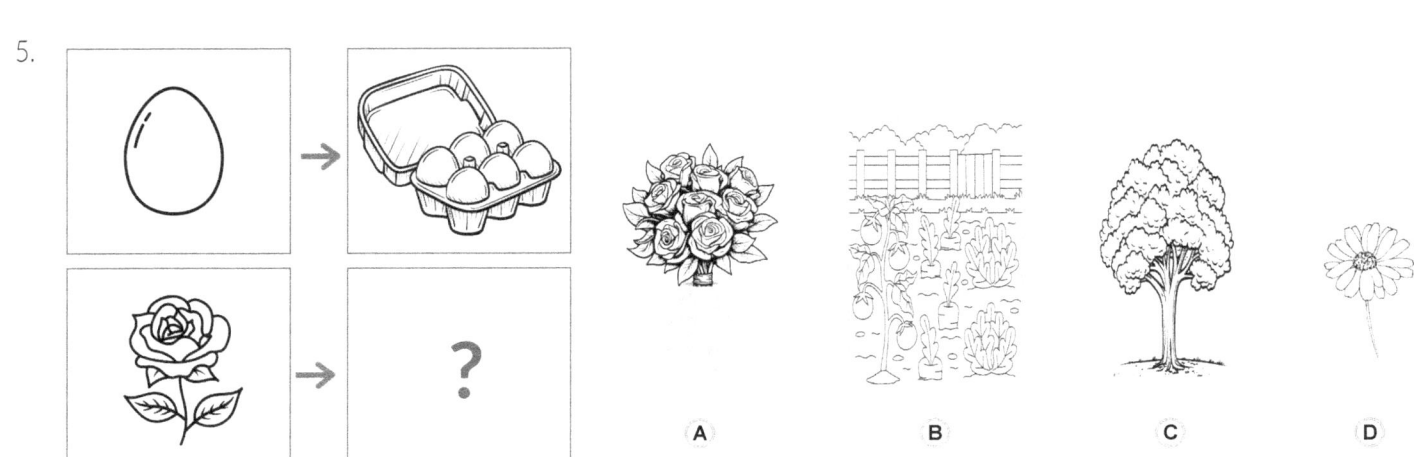

A   B   C   D

6.

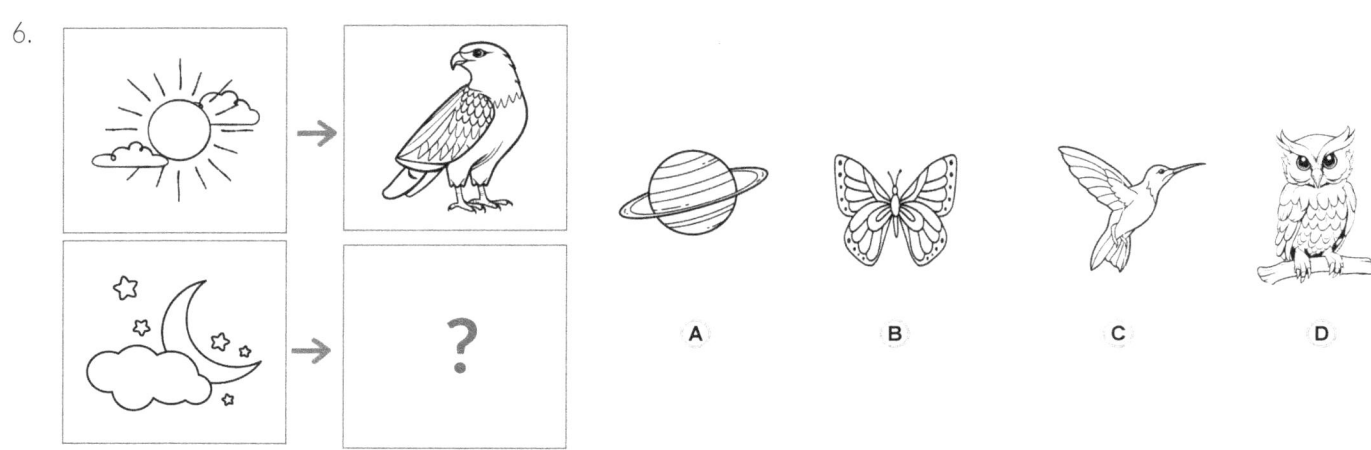

A   B   C   D

7.

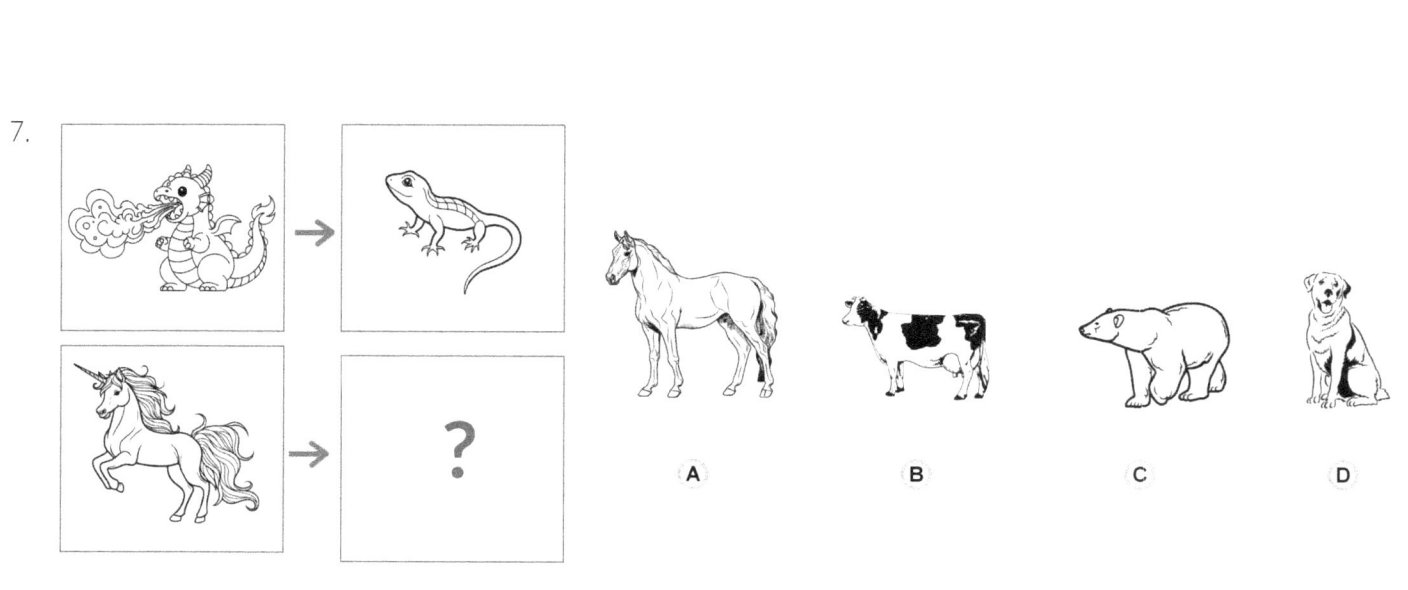

A   B   C   D

8.

| | | A | B | C | D |

9.

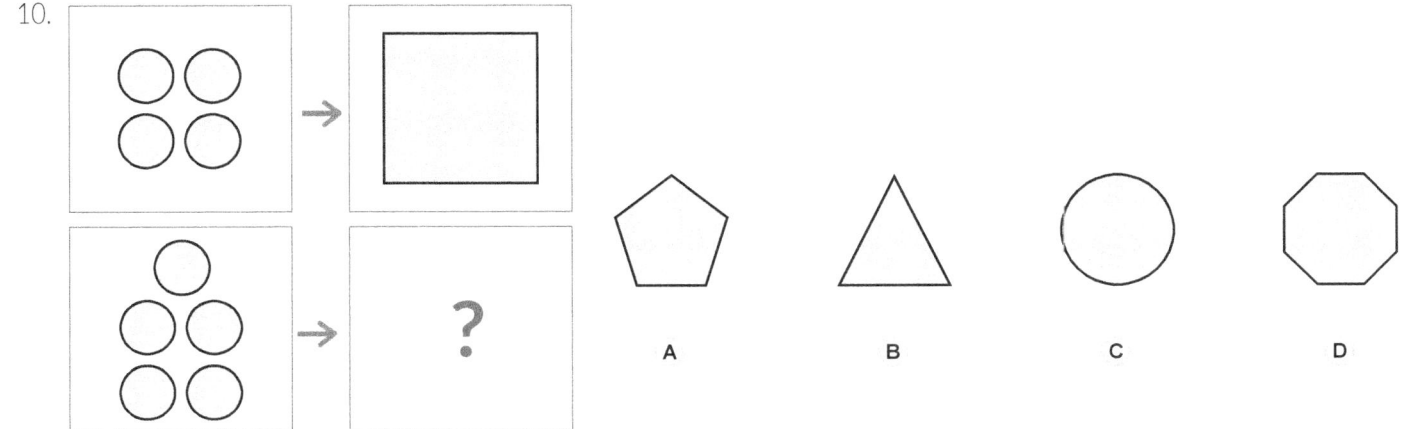

10.

11.

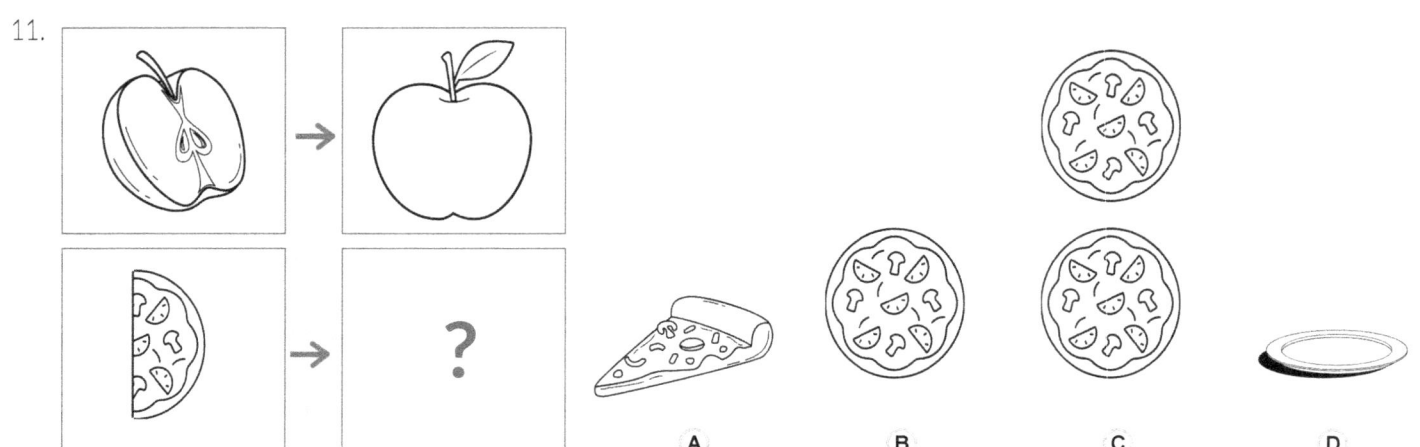

12.

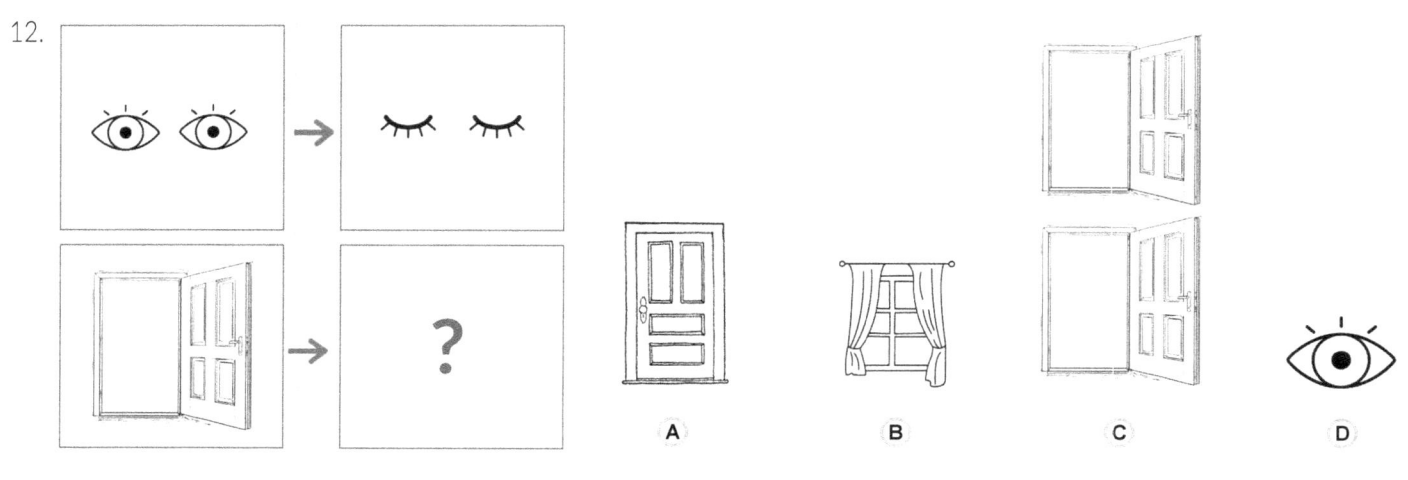

13.

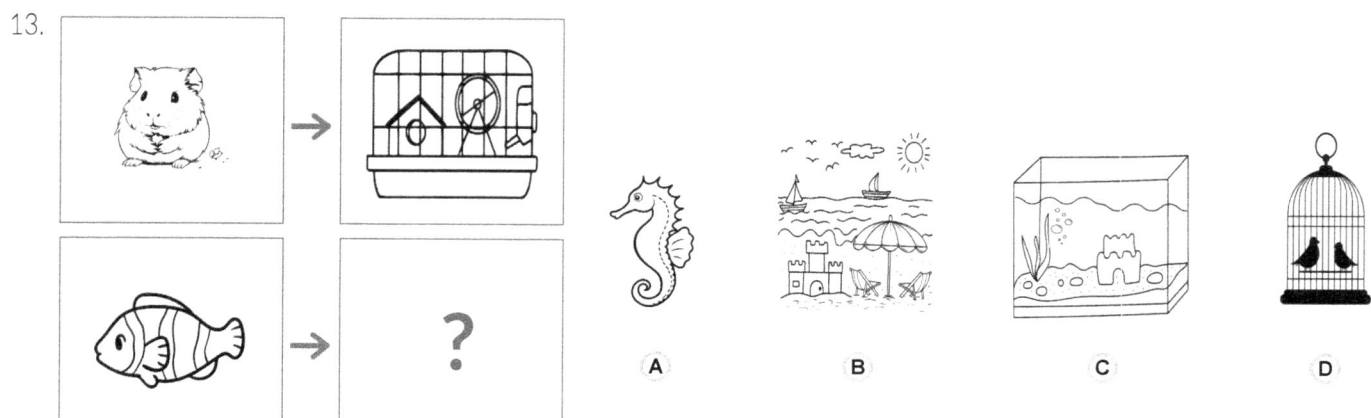

16

14.

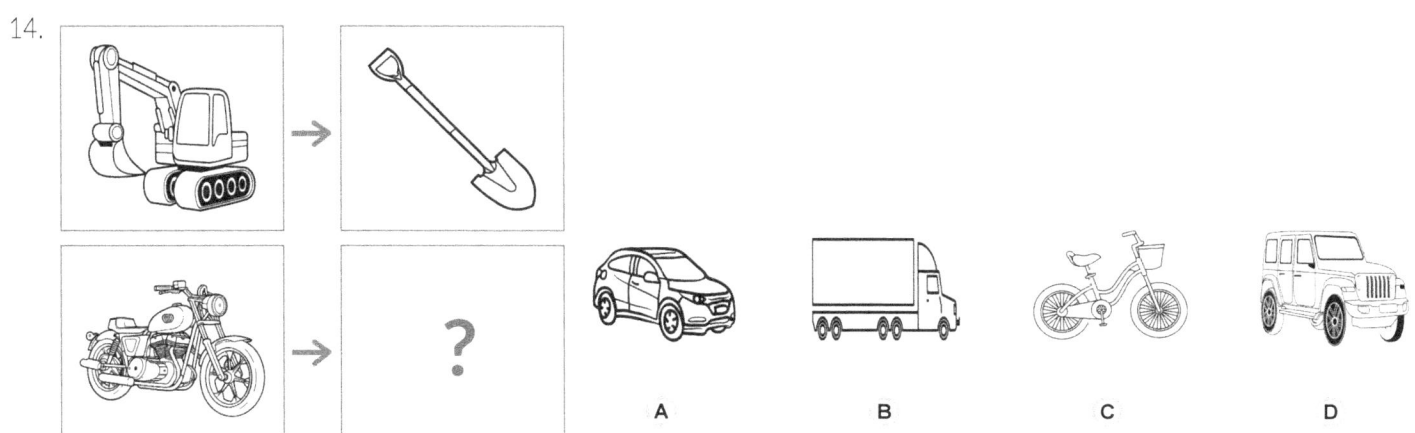

A   B   C   D

15.

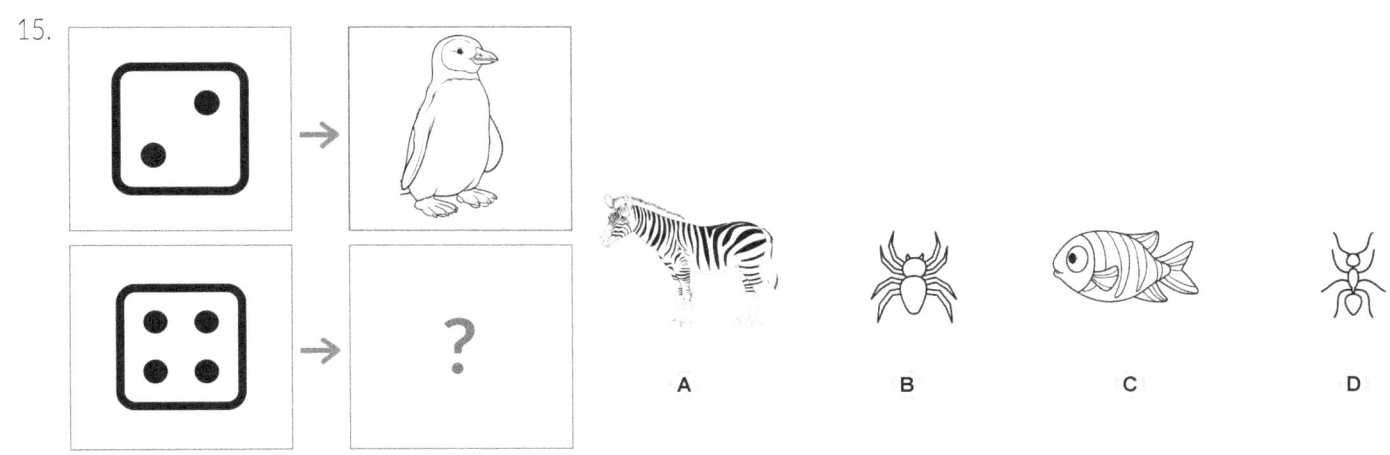

A   B   C   D

16.

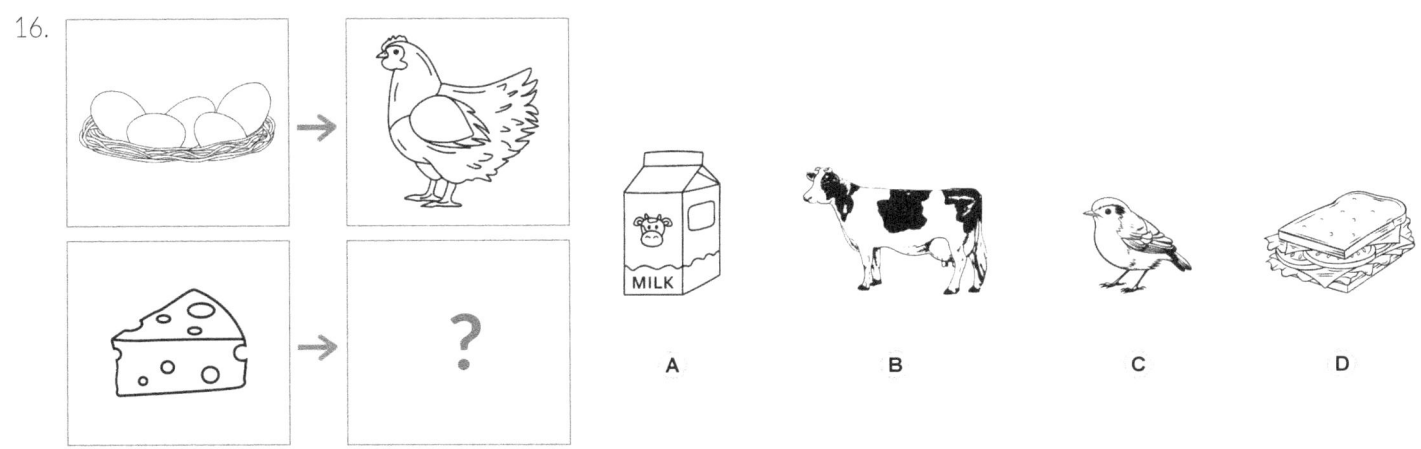

A   B   C   D

17.

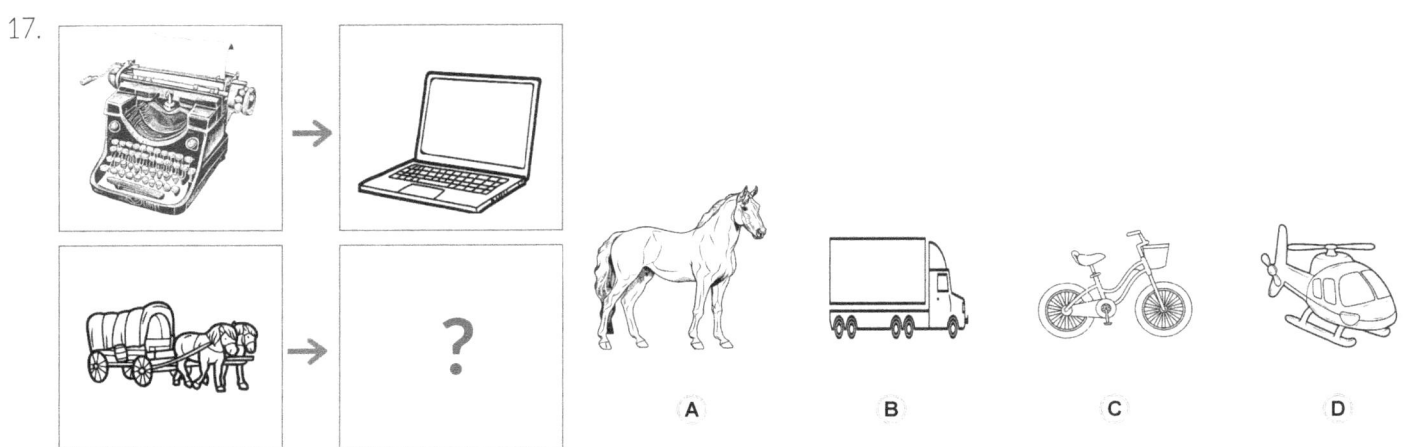

A   B   C   D

18.

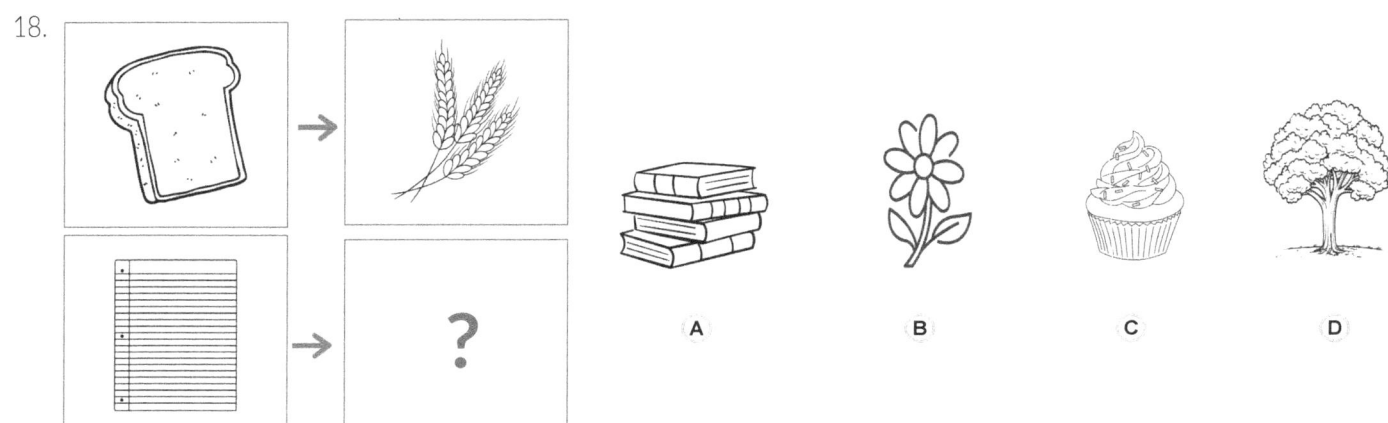

A   B   C   D

Keep up the good work!

Jay

PICTURE CLASSIFICATION

Which one goes best?

Kai

Directions (read to child):
The top row shows three pictures that are alike in some way. Look at the bottom row.
There are four pictures. Which picture in the bottom row goes best with the pictures in the top row?

Explanation (for parents):
A more detailed explanation and another Picture Classification example question are on p.8. If you have not already, look over p.8. Following is an excerpt. Together with your child, try to figure out a "rule" describing how the top pictures are alike and belong together. Then, apply the "rule" to each answer choice to determine which one follows it. If your child finds that more than one choice follows the rule, then a more specific rule is needed.

Example (read to child):
Let's look at the pictures on the top row. We see a violin, a saxophone, and a cello. Let's come up with a "rule" to describe how these are each alike or how they belong together.

These are instruments. Now, look at the bottom row. Let's find the answer choice on the bottom that follows this same rule of things that are instruments. We see a table, a fridge, a spoon, and a piano.

Which one of these goes best with the top row? Which one of them is an instrument? The piano.

1.

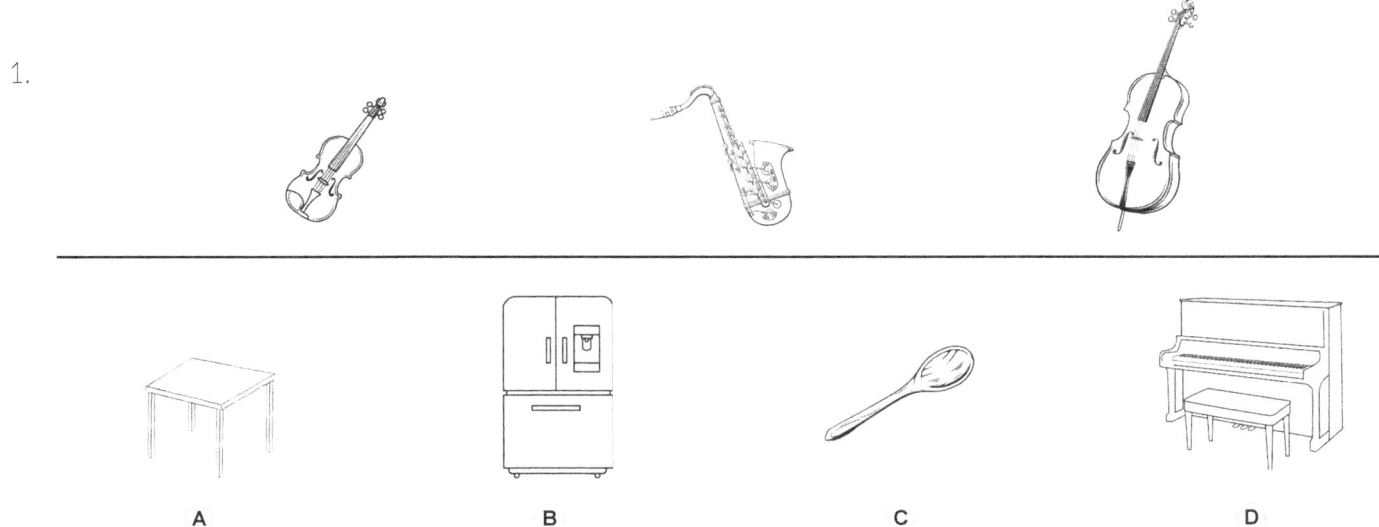

A   B   C   D

2.

 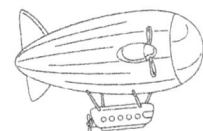 

  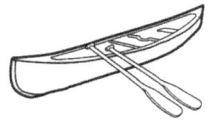 

A   B   C   D

3.

A   B   C   D

4.

A   B   C   D

5.

A   B   C   D

6.

A   B   C   D

7.

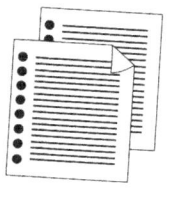   

A   B   C   D

8.

  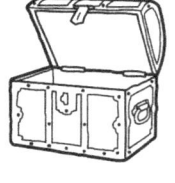 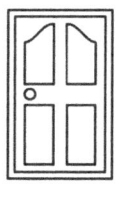

A   B   C   D

9.

A   B   C   D

10.   E   O   U

N   P   I   B

A   B   C   D

11.

A   B   C   D

12.

A   B   C   D

13.

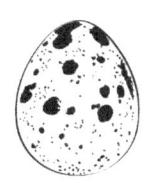  

A   B   C   D

23

14.

  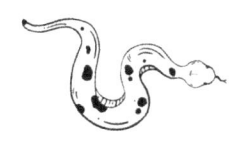 

A   B   C   D

15.

A   B   C   D

16.

A   B   C   D

17.

  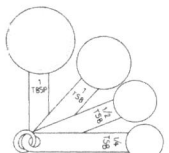

A

B

C

D

18.

A

B

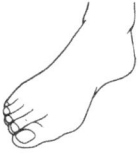

C

D

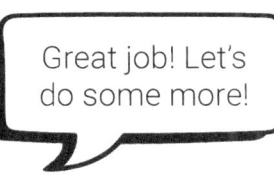
Great job! Let's do some more!

Emma

SENTENCE COMPLETION

Maya

Listen closely!

Directions (read to child): Listen to the question, then choose the best answer. I can only read the question one time.

Additional information (for parents): Read the questions in this section to your child.

As explained earlier in the Introduction on p. 10, test administrators will read these questions only one time.

Therefore, it is imperative that your child practice careful listening skills, so that you will not need to repeat the questions.

1. Which of these people helps put out fires?

    A   B   C   D

2. In science class, if you were learning about animals that hibernate, which one of these could you be learning about?

    A   B   C   D

3. If you were in a dentist's office, which one of these would you most likely see?

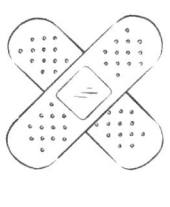

A

B

C

D

4. Which of these would a violinist play?

A

B

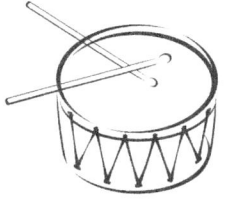

C

D

5. At the supermarket, you see the 4 foods below. Which one would have the most seeds?

A

B

C

D

6. If you were a baker, which one of these would you use while at work?

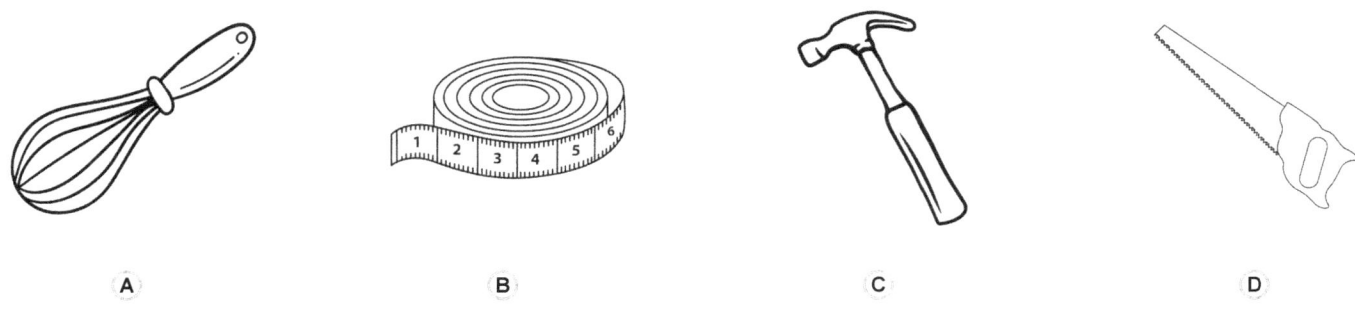

A   B   C   D

7. Your class is doing an craft project. Some of the items you used are: something for cutting, something for coloring, and something for measuring. Which picture shows these 3 things?

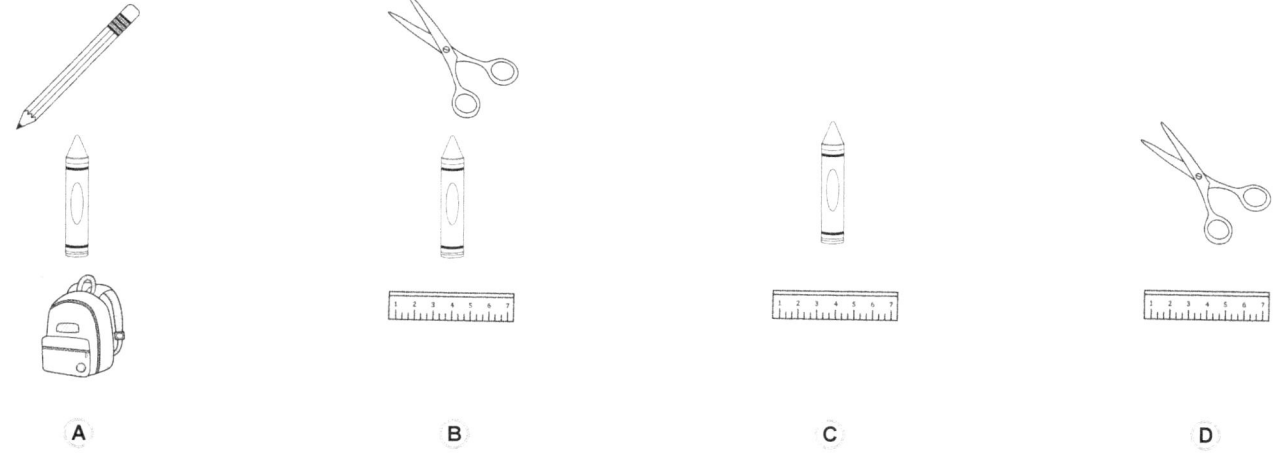

A   B   C   D

8. Which one of these places would have the coldest temperatures year-round?

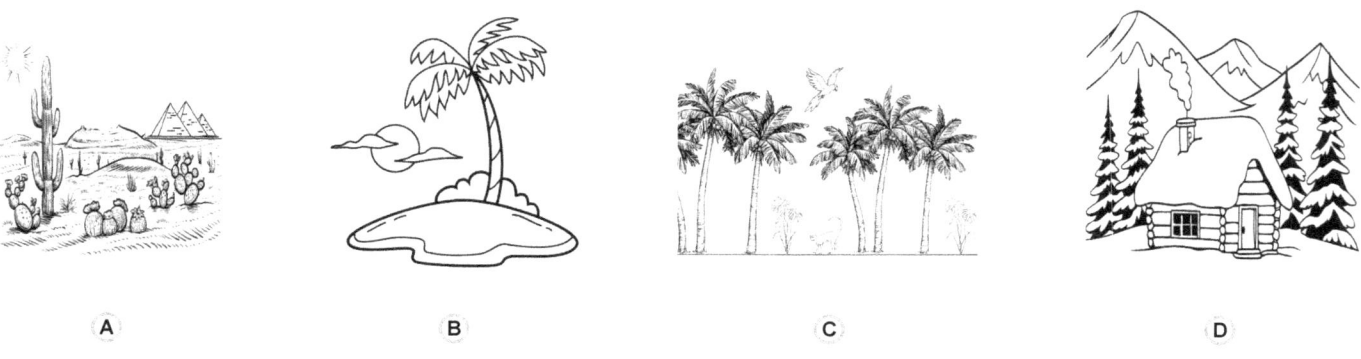

A   B   C   D

9. If the water stopped running in your house, which one of these would no longer work?

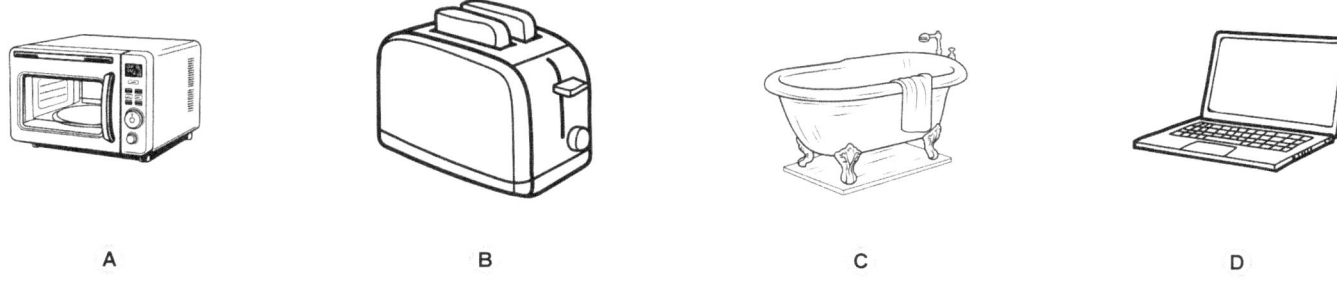

A   B   C   D

10. You are reading a book about an animal that does not grow legs. Which animal is your book about?

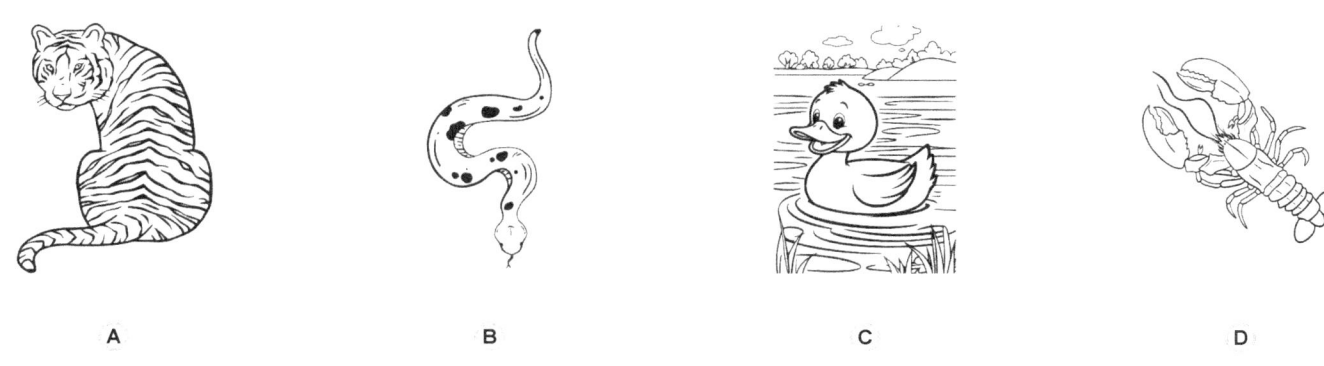

A   B   C   D

11. Your teacher says you will learn about something prehistoric. Which one of these are you most likely going to learn about?

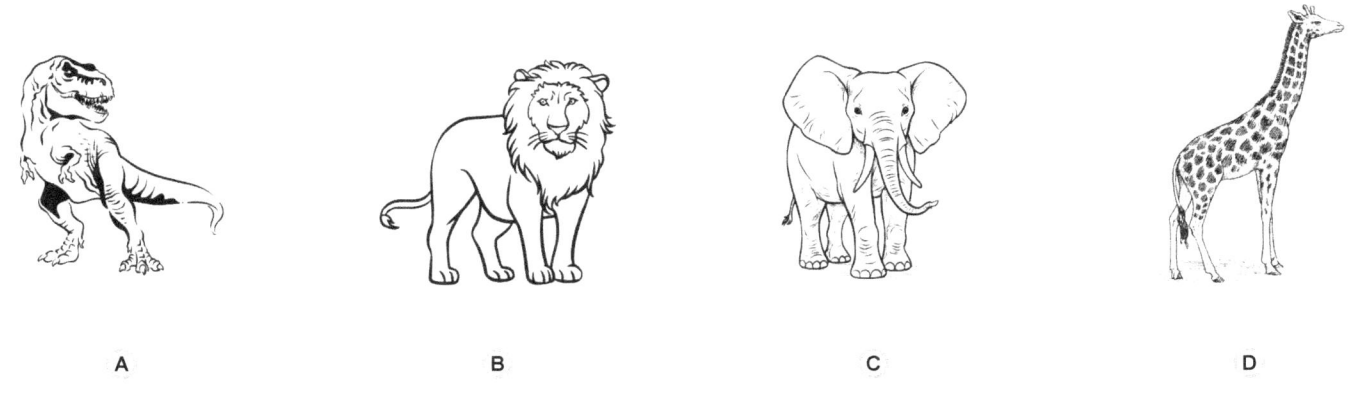

A   B   C   D

12. Which picture shows three things found in the ocean and one thing found on land?

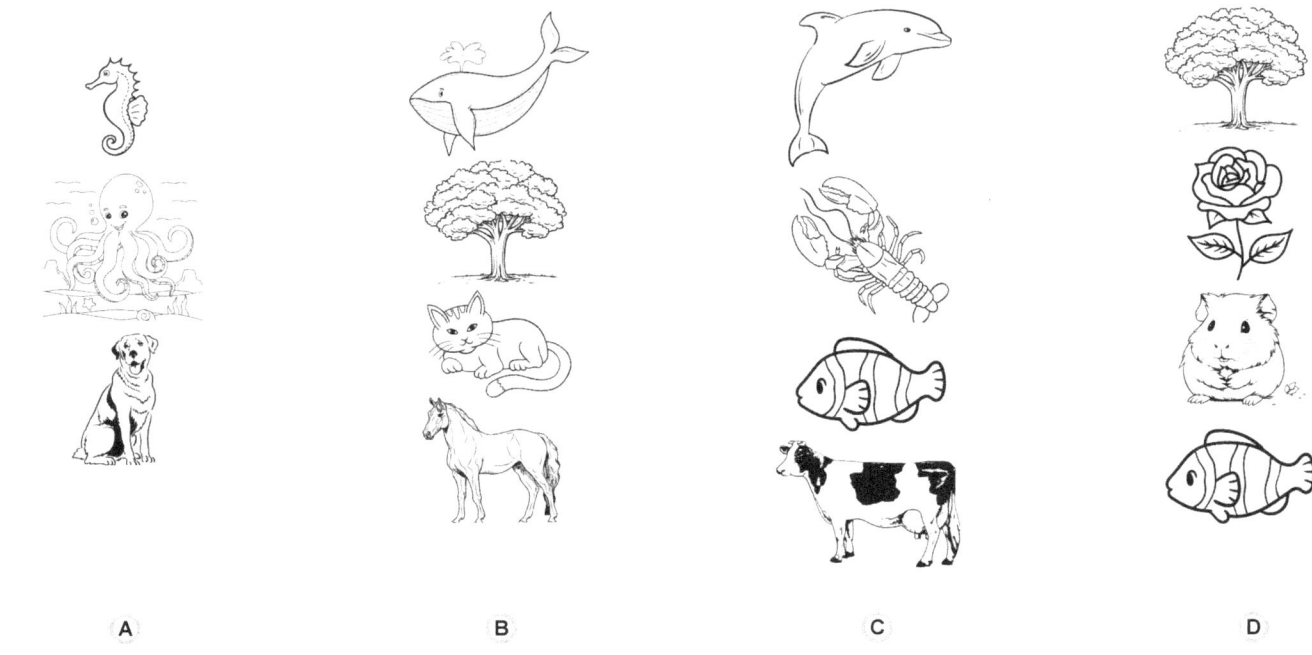

A   B   C   D

13. Your cousin is going somewhere tropical on vacation. Which picture shows where they probably are going?

A   B   C   D

14. You are watching a video about something modern. Which one of these could the video be about?

A   B   C   D

15. Your friend's favorite fruit is one that grows on a tree. Which picture shows your friend's favorite fruit?

A   B   C   D

16. Which one of the objects below would be the coldest?

A   B   C   D

- End of Practice Test 1 (Workbook Format) -

Excellent job! You're done with the first part!

Zoe

COGAT® PRACTICE TEST 2

START OF PRACTICE TEST 2 / PICTURE ANALOGIES

Directions: The pictures in the top boxes go together in some way. One of the bottom boxes is empty. Which answer choice goes with the picture in the bottom box in the same way the top pictures do?

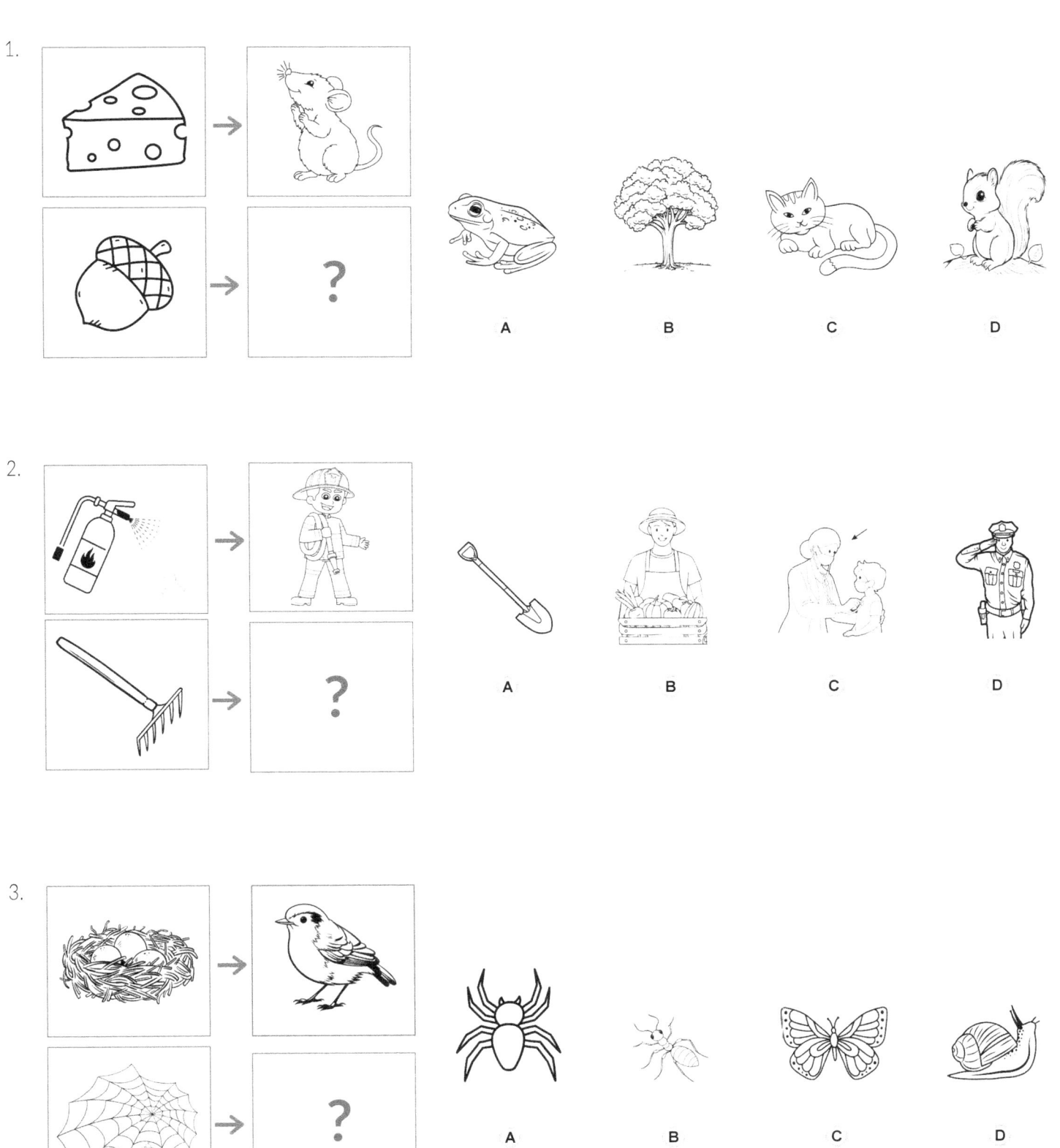

1.

A   B   C   D

2.

A   B   C   D

3.

A   B   C   D

4.

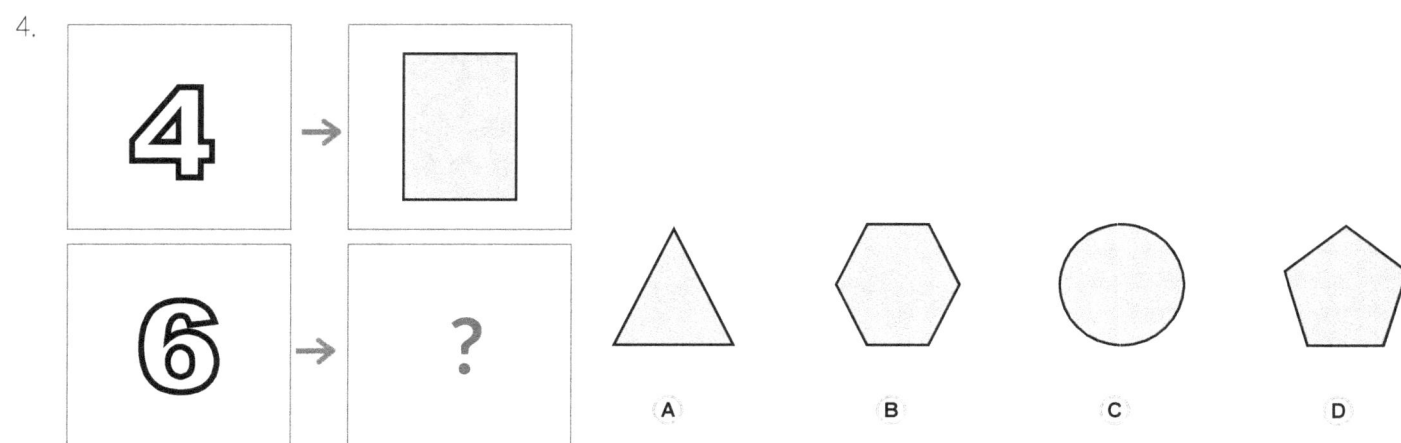

5.

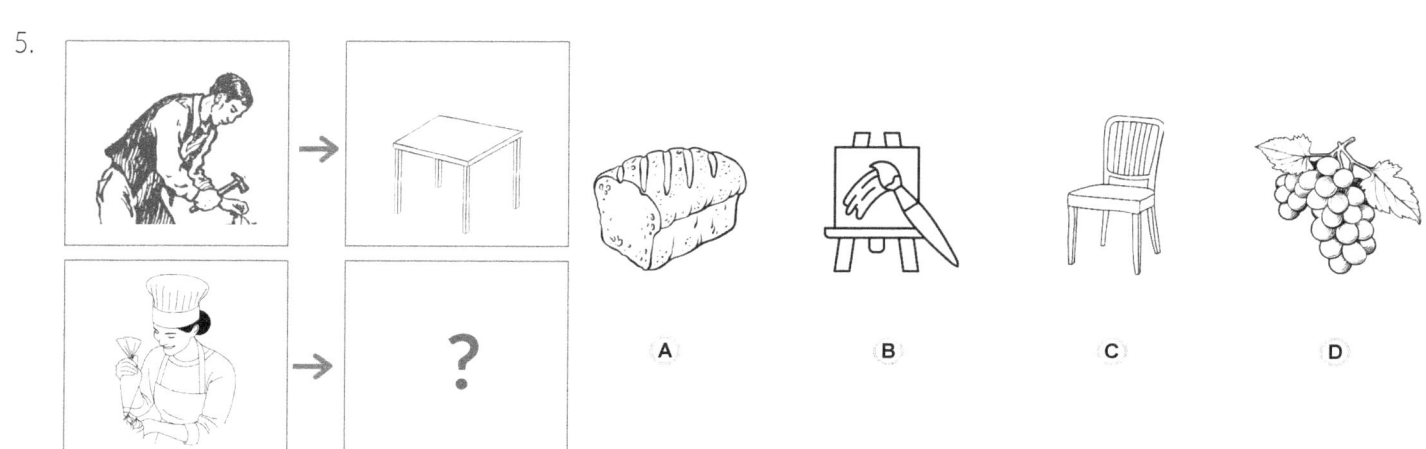

6.

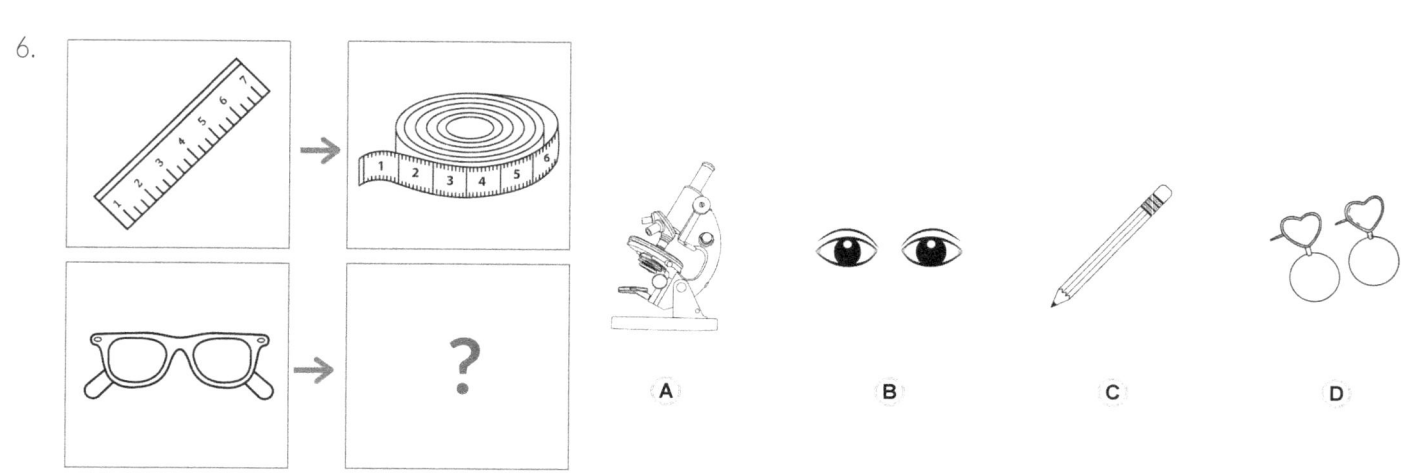

34

7.

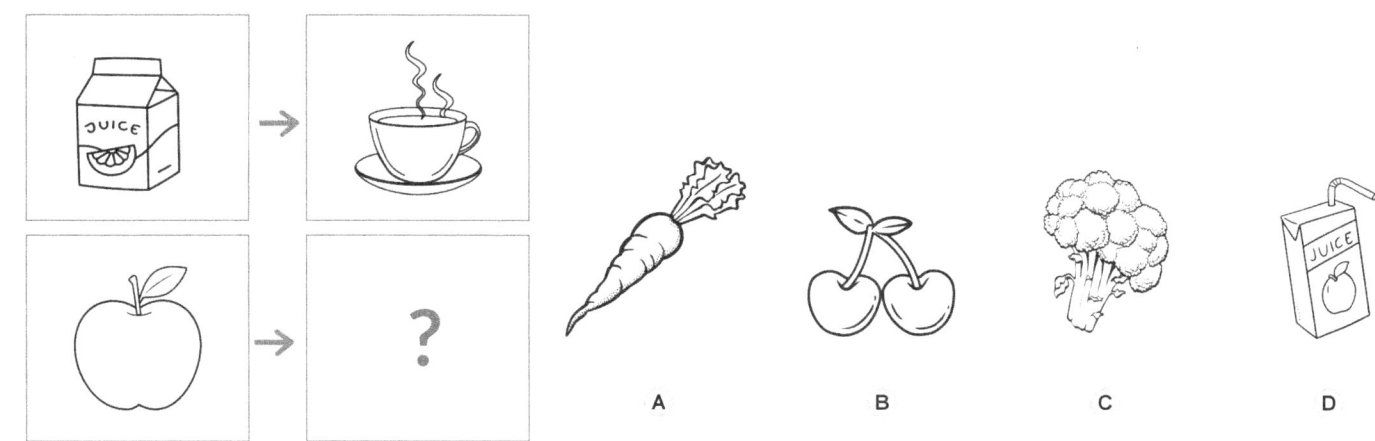

A B C D

8.

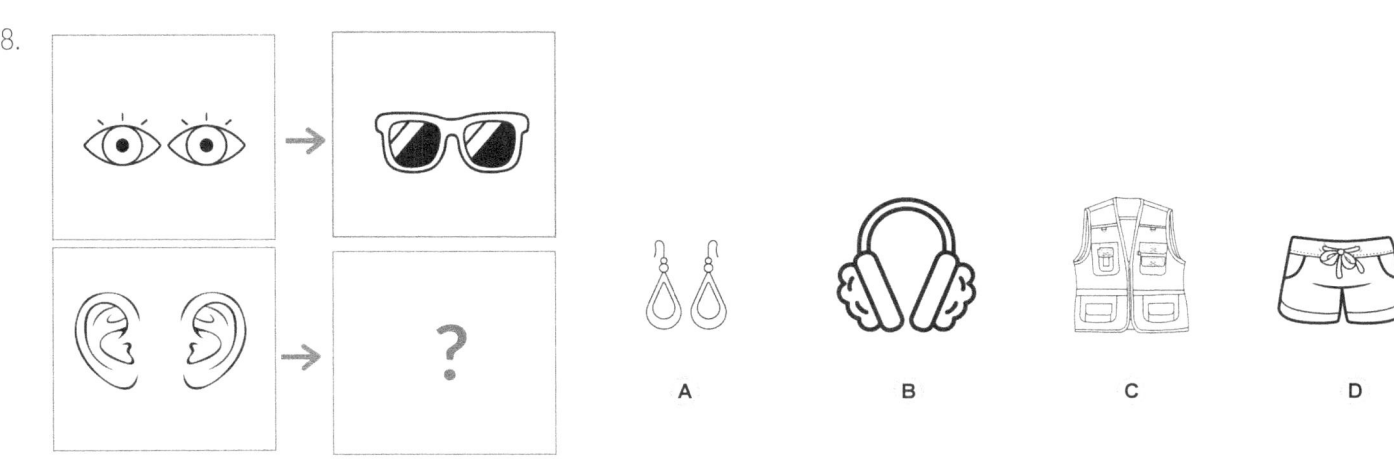

A B C D

9.

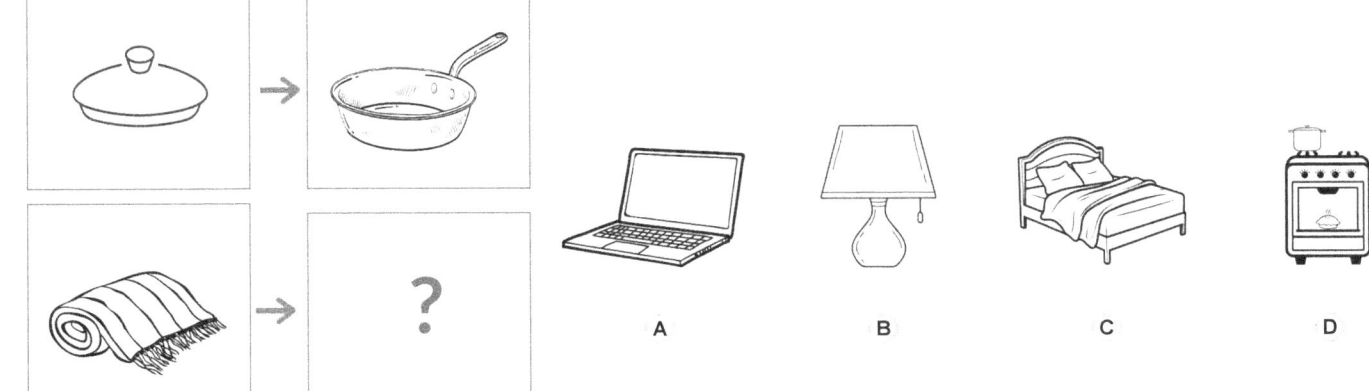

A B C D

10.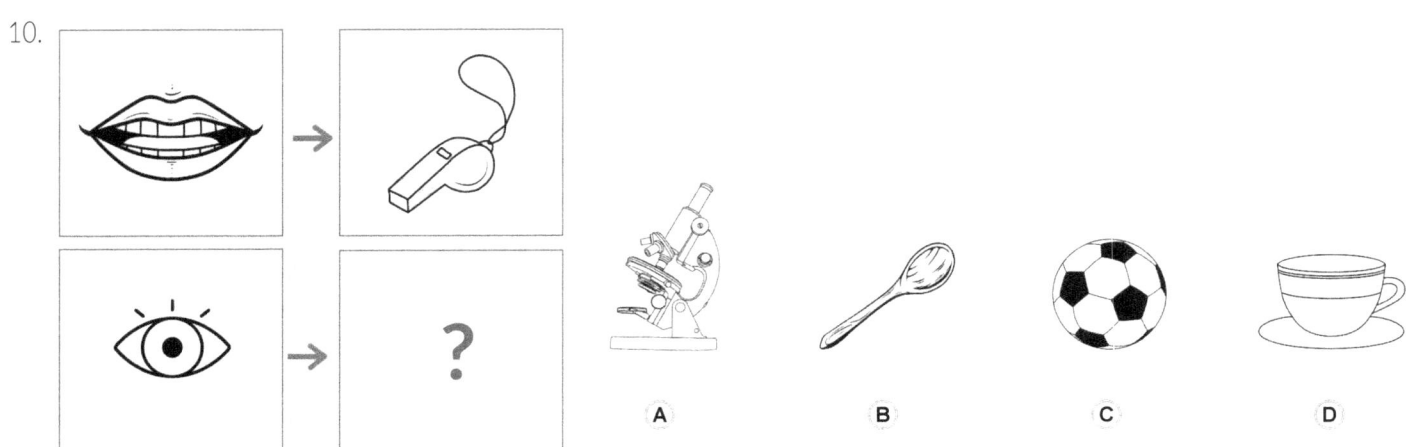

11.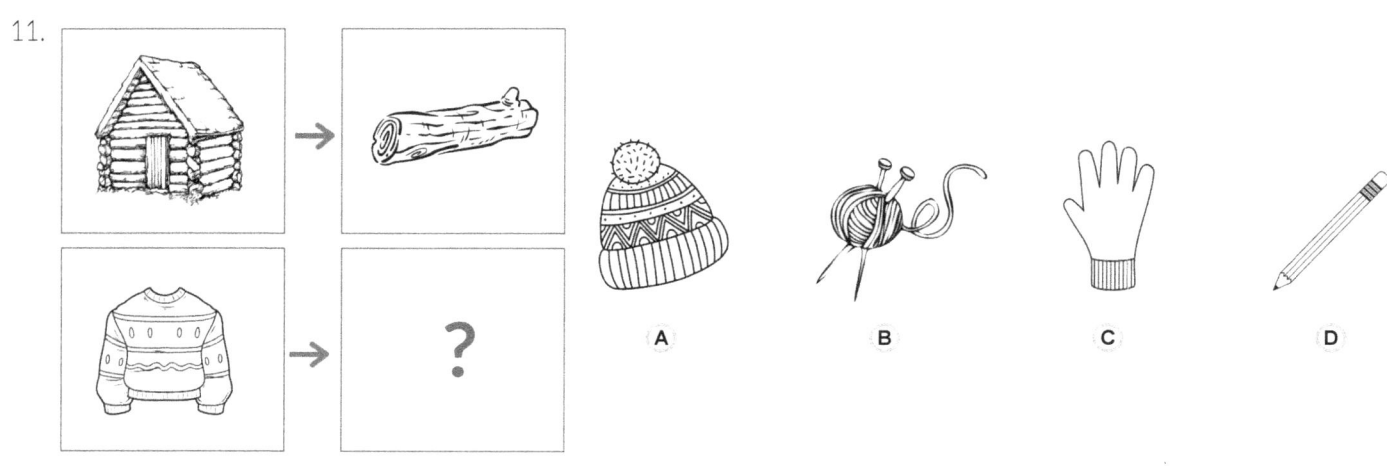

12.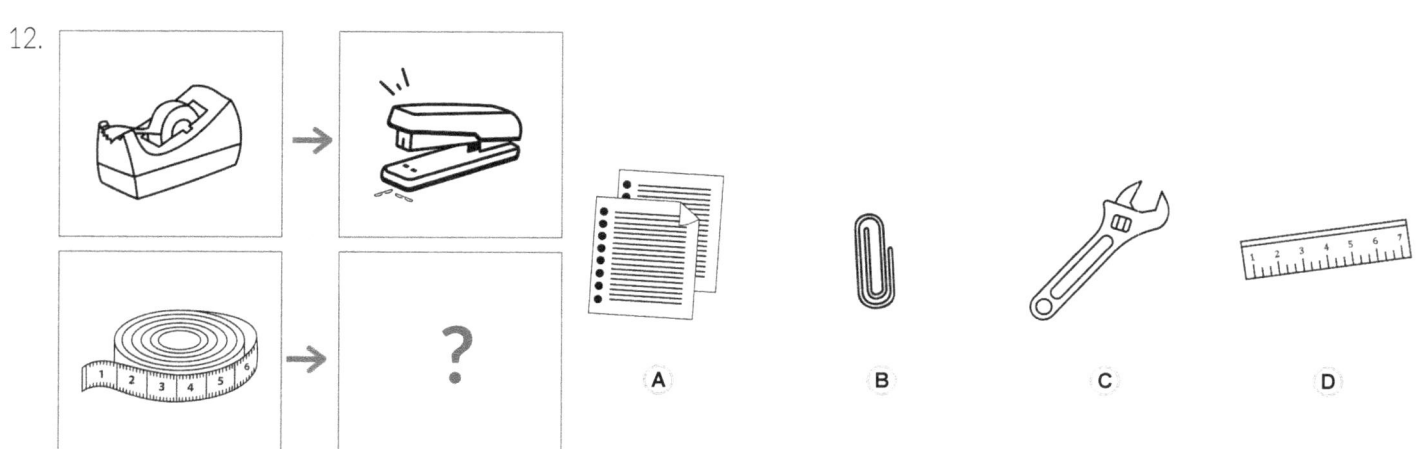

36

13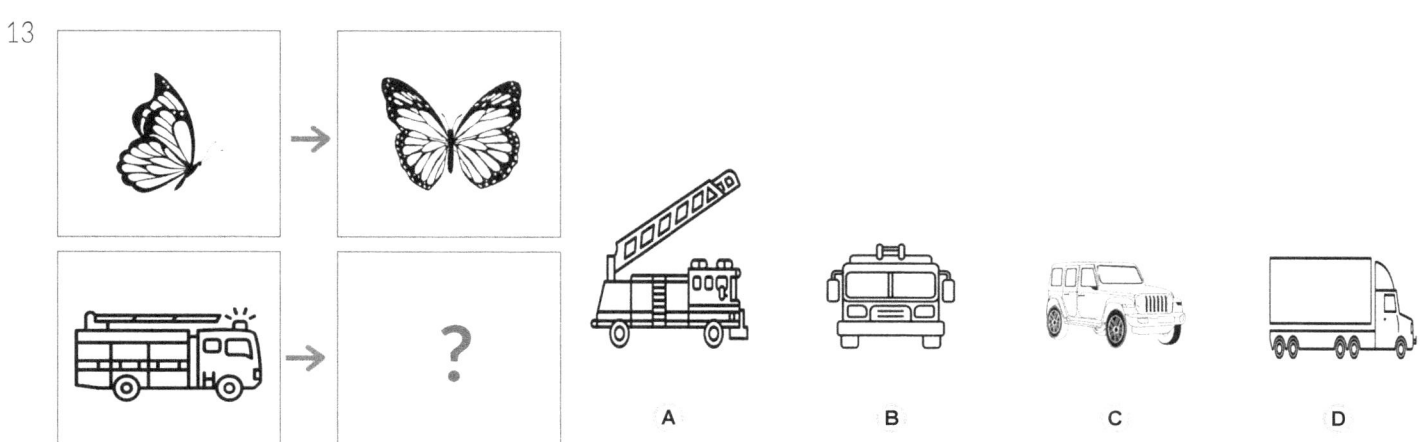

14.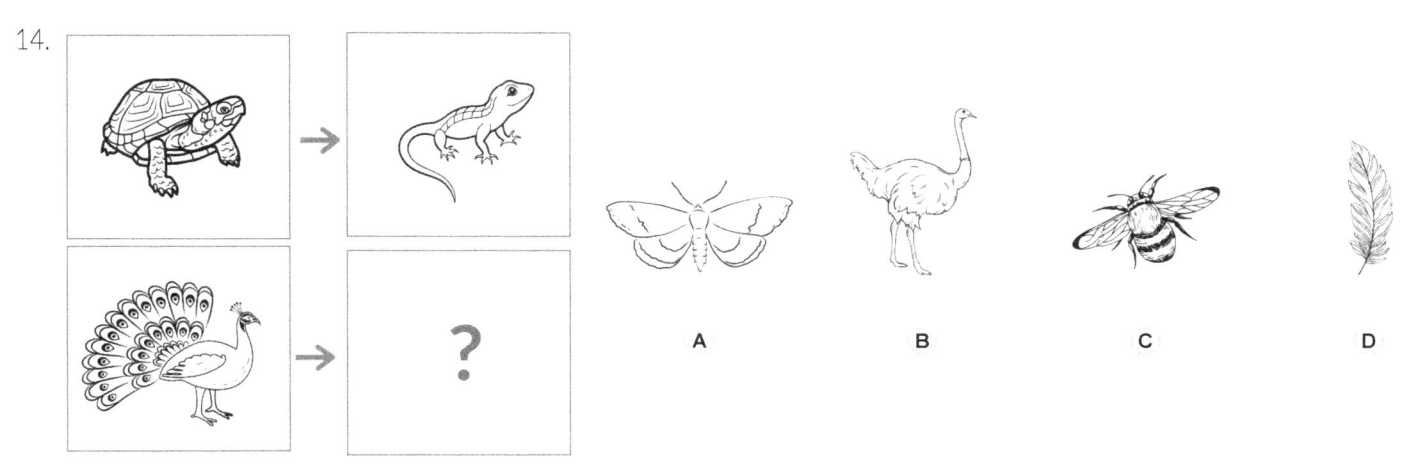

15.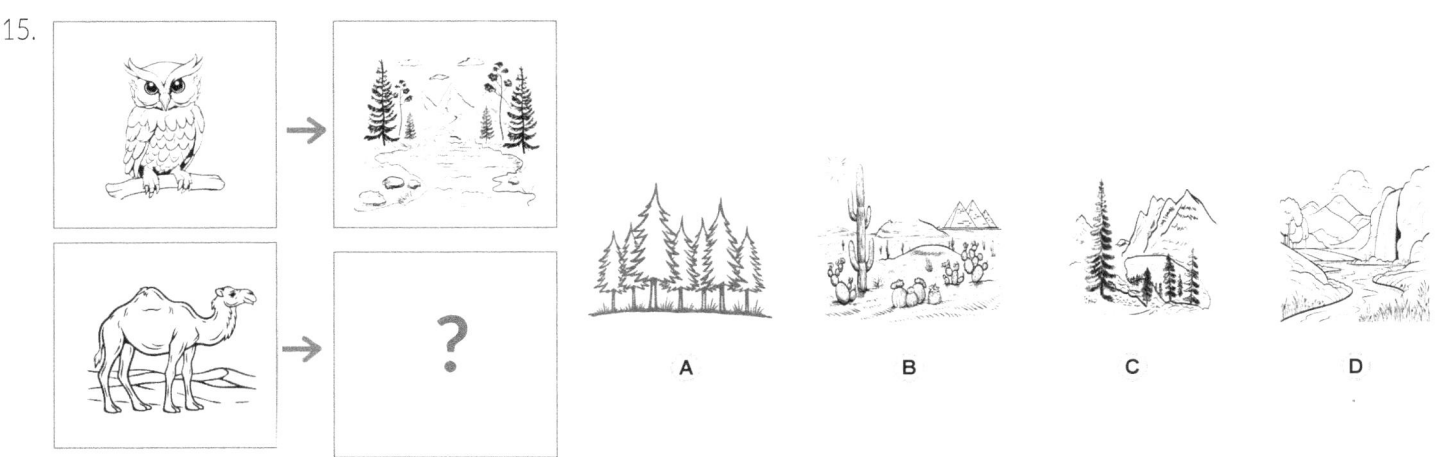

16.

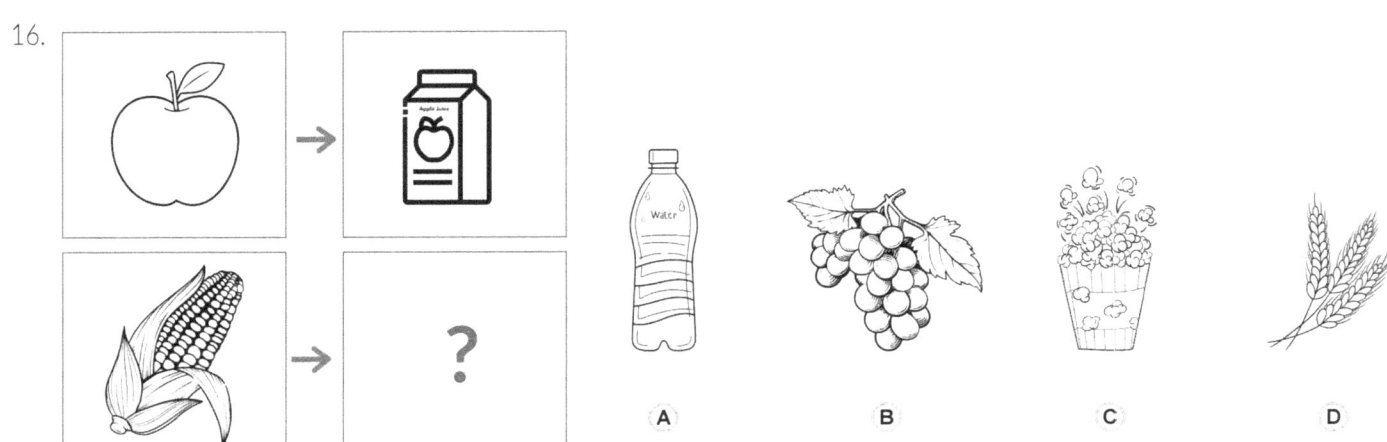

A   B   C   D

17.

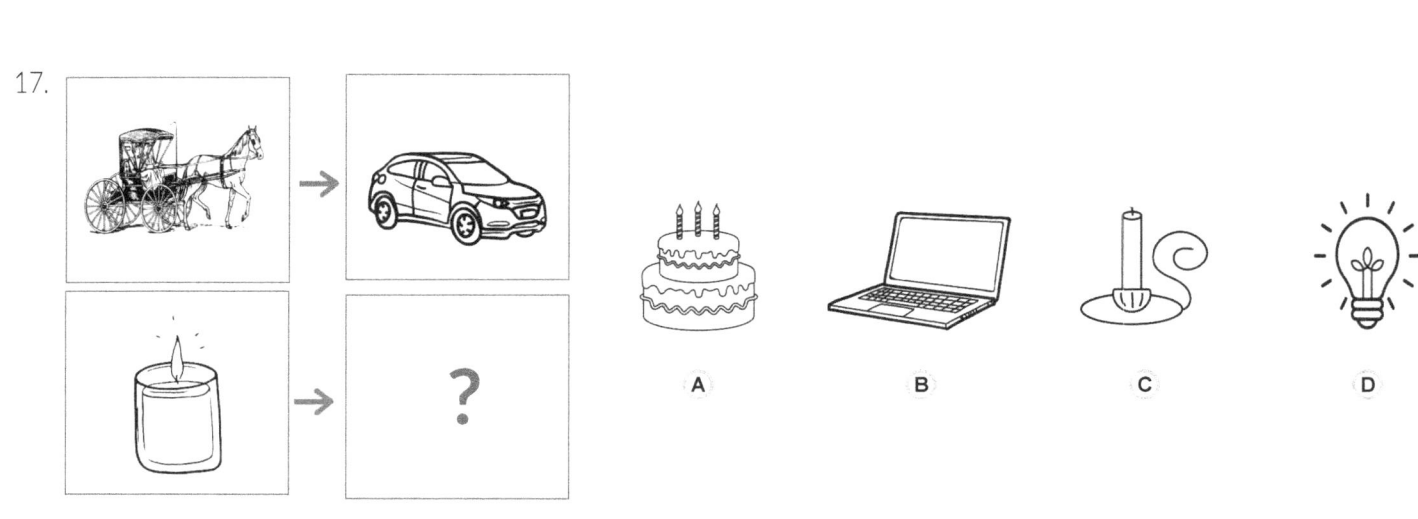

A   B   C   D

18.

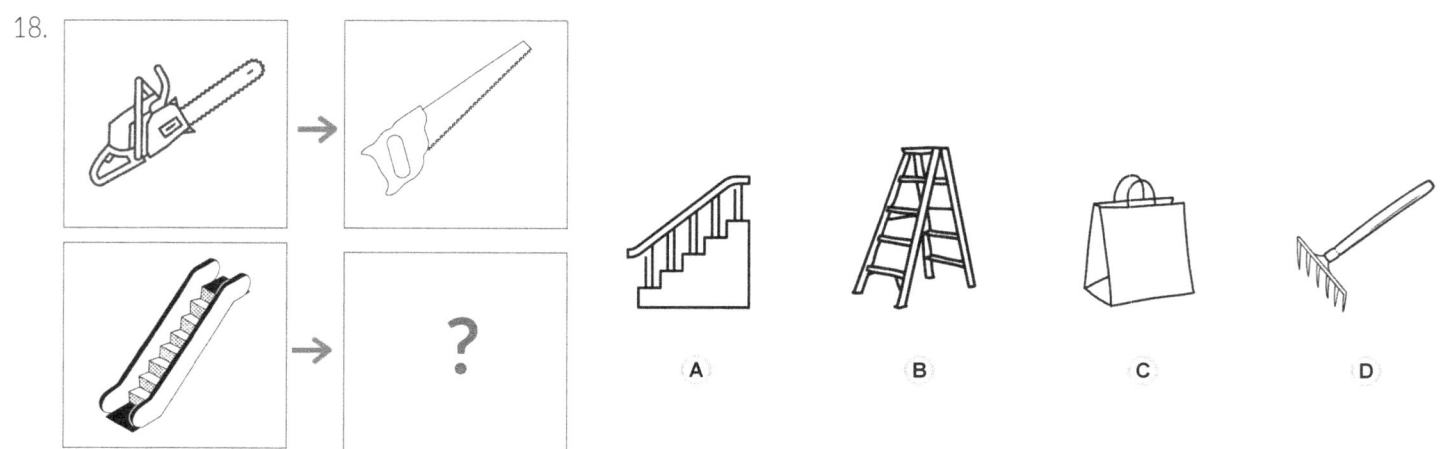

A   B   C   D

PICTURE CLASSIFICATION
Directions: The top row shows three pictures that are alike in some way. Look at the bottom row. Which bottom picture goes best with the top pictures?

1.

2.

3.

4.

  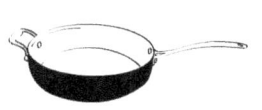

 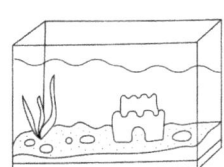  

A B C D

5.

A B C D

6.

A B C D

7.

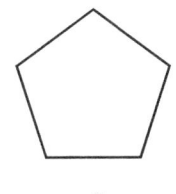

A   B   C   D

8.

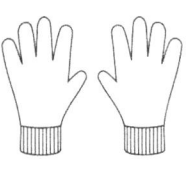

A   B   C   D

9.

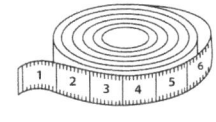

A   B   C   D

10.

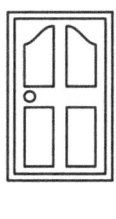 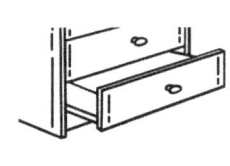  

(A) (B) (C) (D)

11.

(A) (B) (C) (D)

12.

A B C D

13.

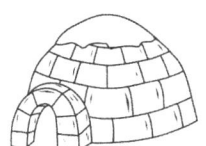  

___

A   B   C   D

14.

  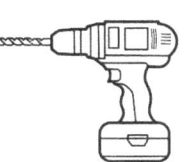

___

A   B   C   D

15.

  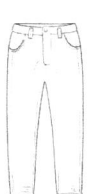

___

 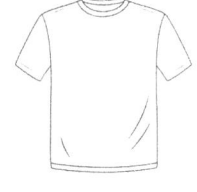 

A   B   C   D

16.

    A   **B**   **C**   **D**

17.

  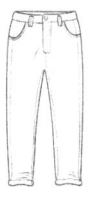 

    A   **B**   **C**   **D**

18.

  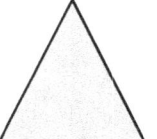

    A   **B**   **C**   **D**

SENTENCE COMPLETION

Directions: Listen to the question, then choose the best answer.

1. If you were going to a summer picnic, which of these would you wear?

A

B

C

D

2. Which item would you not find in a classroom?

A

B

C

D

3. Which picture shows something that often comes in pairs?

A

B

C

D

4. If you were doing a science experiment in a lab, which of these would you most likely use?

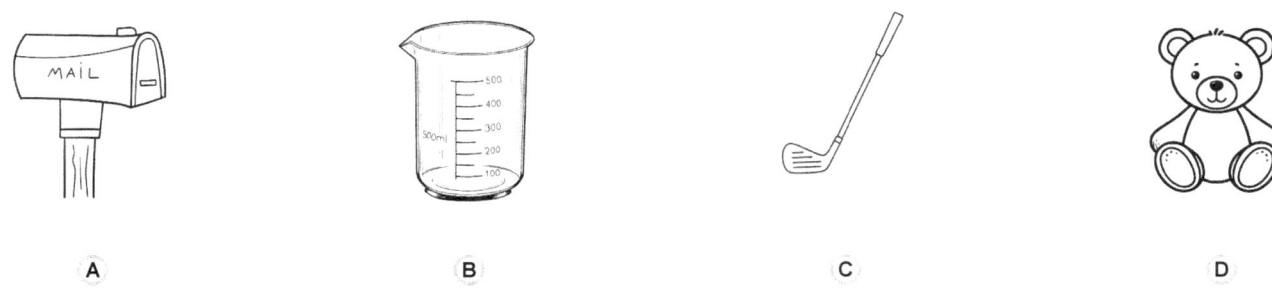

A   B   C   D

5. Which picture shows 2 objects that are used for cooking?

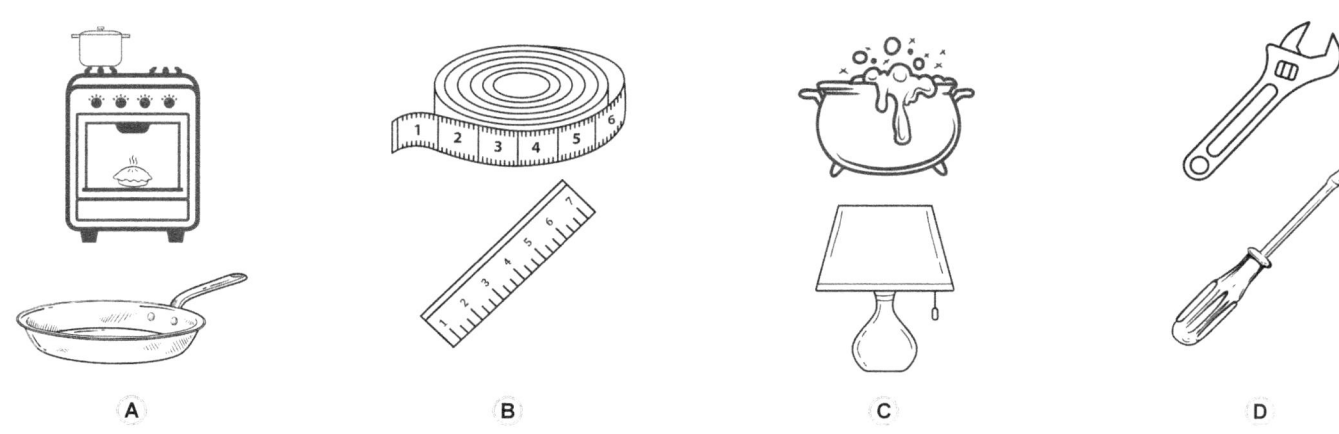

A   B   C   D

6. In the shapes below, the shapes stand for different types of fruit. A circle stands for an apple. A triangle stands for a banana. Which choice would show 1 apple and 1 banana?

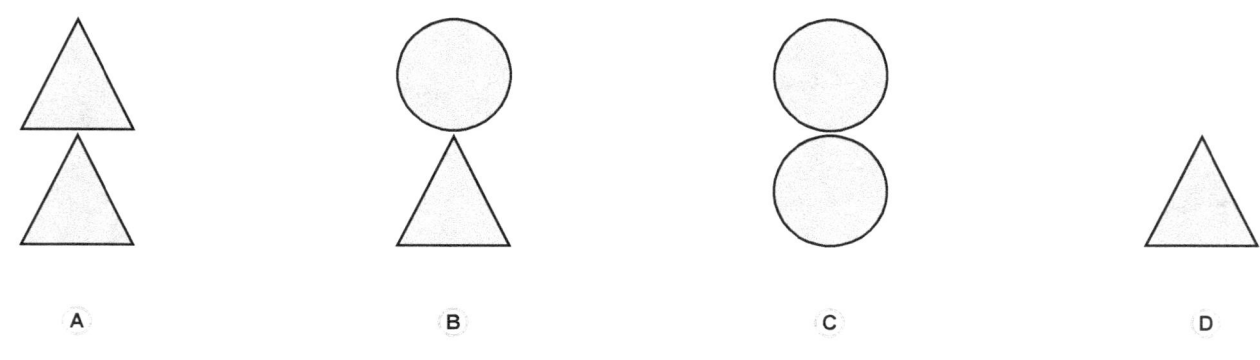

A   B   C   D

7. Which of these shows neither a plant nor a food that comes from an animal?

A   B   C   D

8. Which choice shows 1 animal that lives underwater and 1 animal that can climb trees?

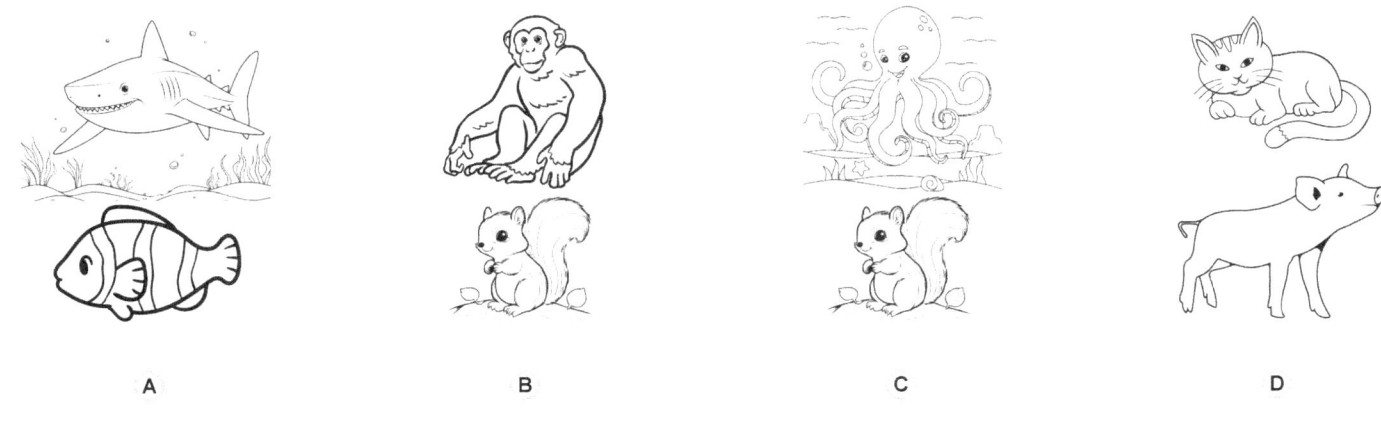

A   B   C   D

9. Which picture shows animals that only live in cold climates?

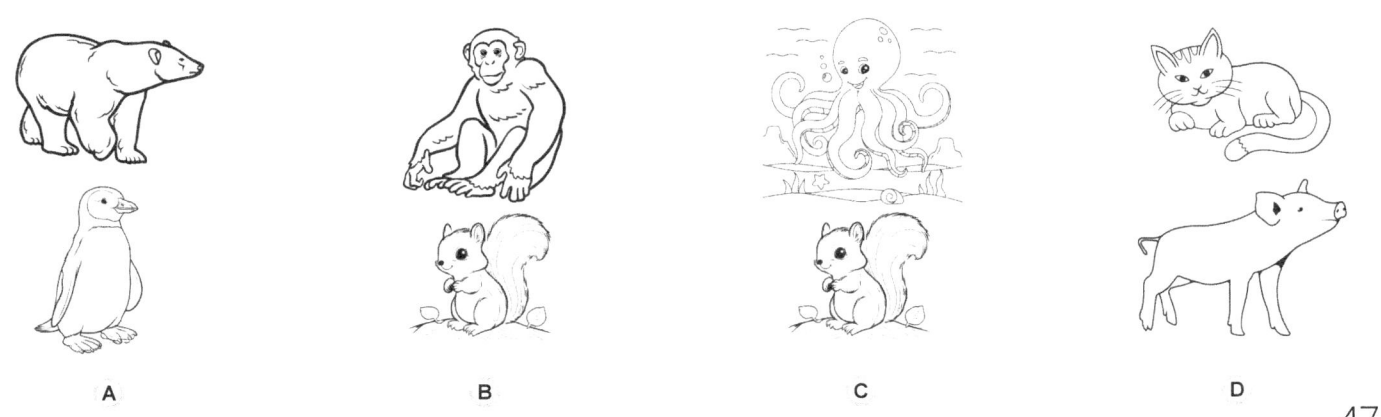

A   B   C   D

10. In class, you are learning about something ancient. Which of these could you be learning about?

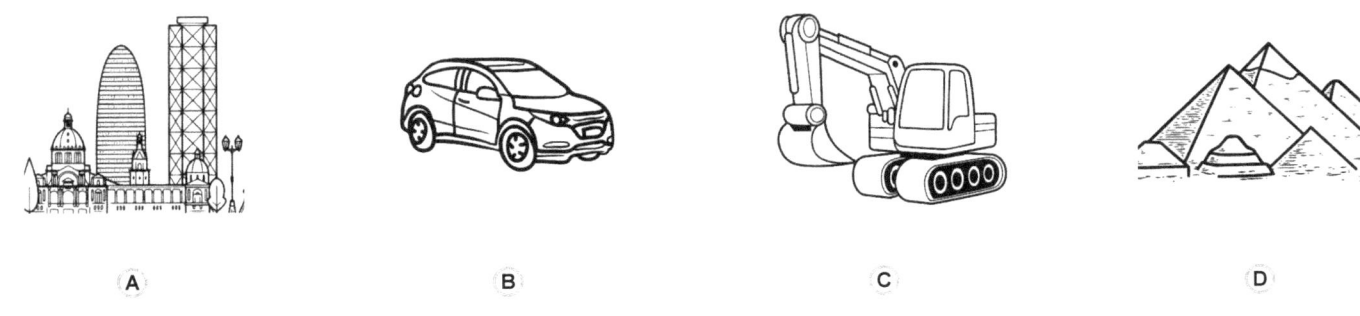

A   B   C   D

11. Which picture shows a food that is made from something that comes from an animal?

A   B   C   D

12. You have to write a story about an animal that lives in a herd. Which choice shows an animal that your story could be about?

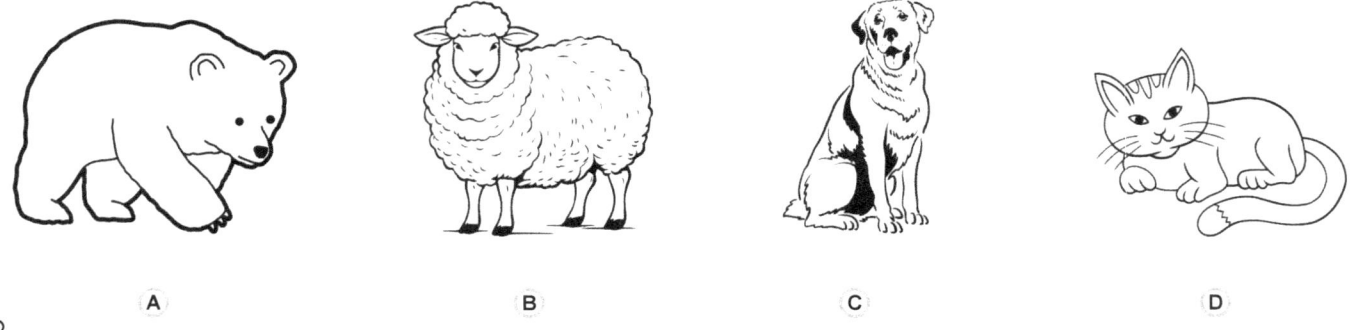

A   B   C   D

13. If there were precipitation, which of these would be the best to have?

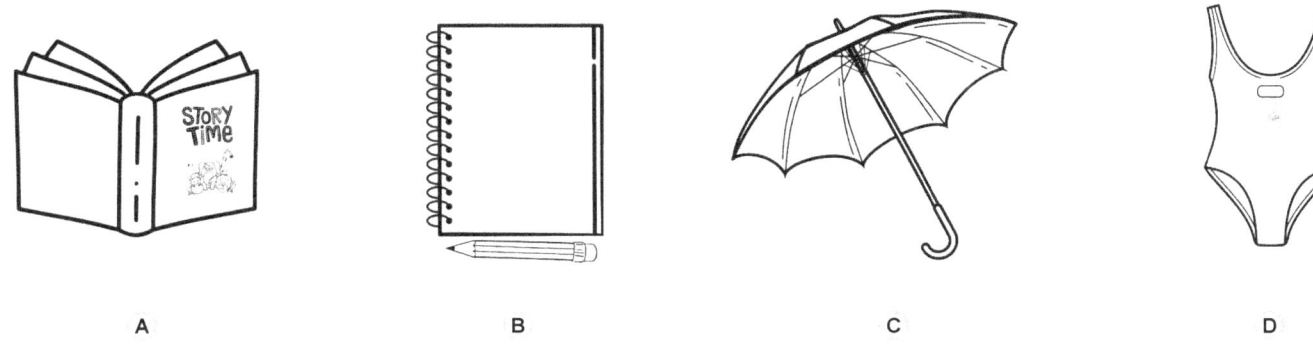

A
B
C
D

14. If you wanted to keep something from being stolen, which one of these would be best to use?

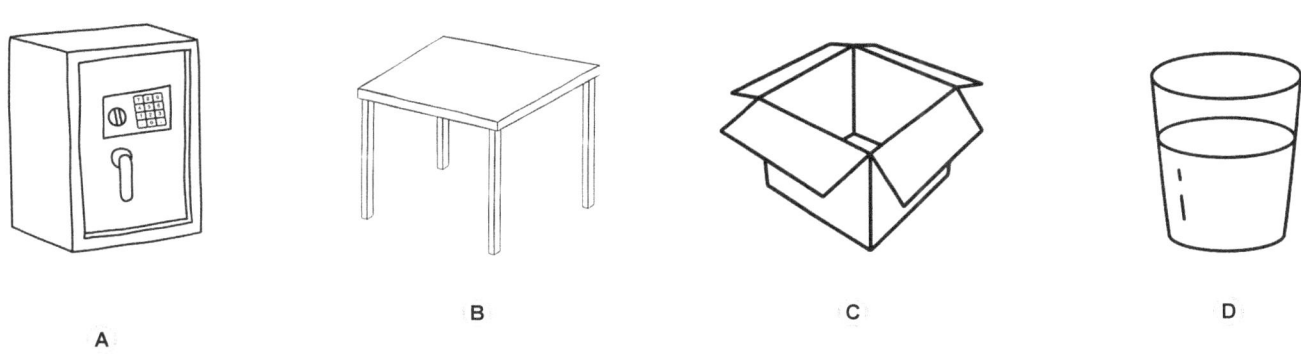

A
B
C
D

15. There are 2 types of food on a table. One is a food picked from a tree. One is a food that grows on a vine. Which picture shows the 2 types of food?

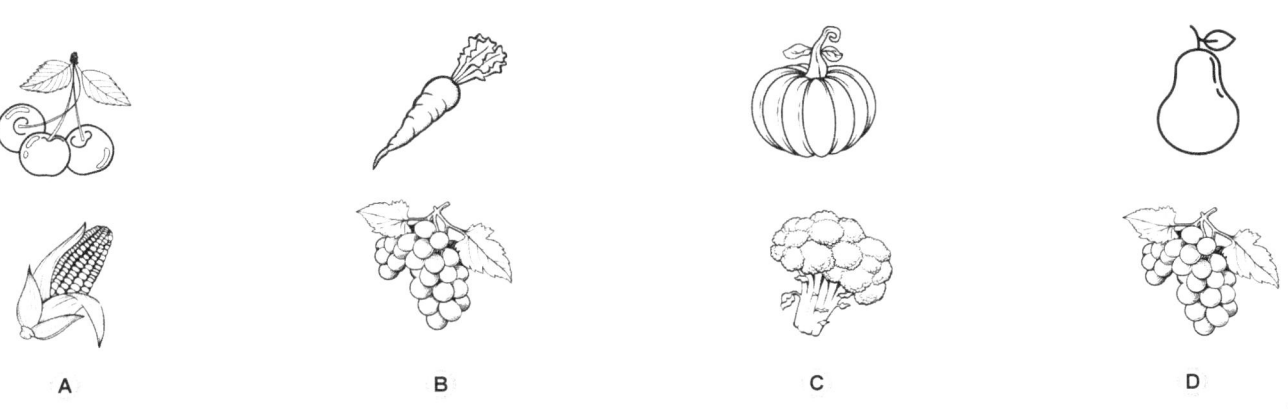

A
B
C
D

16. Which one of these would you not see at a construction site?

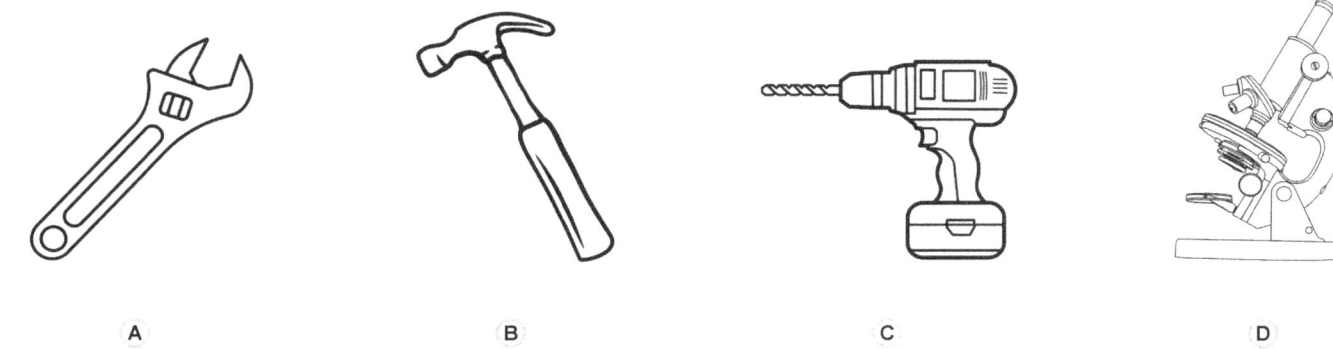

A   B   C   D

- End of Practice Test 2 -

Good job!
You're done with
the second part!

Caleb

COGAT® PRACTICE TEST 3

Directions: The pictures in the top boxes go together in some way. One of the bottom boxes is empty. Which answer choice goes with the picture in the bottom box in the same way the top pictures do?

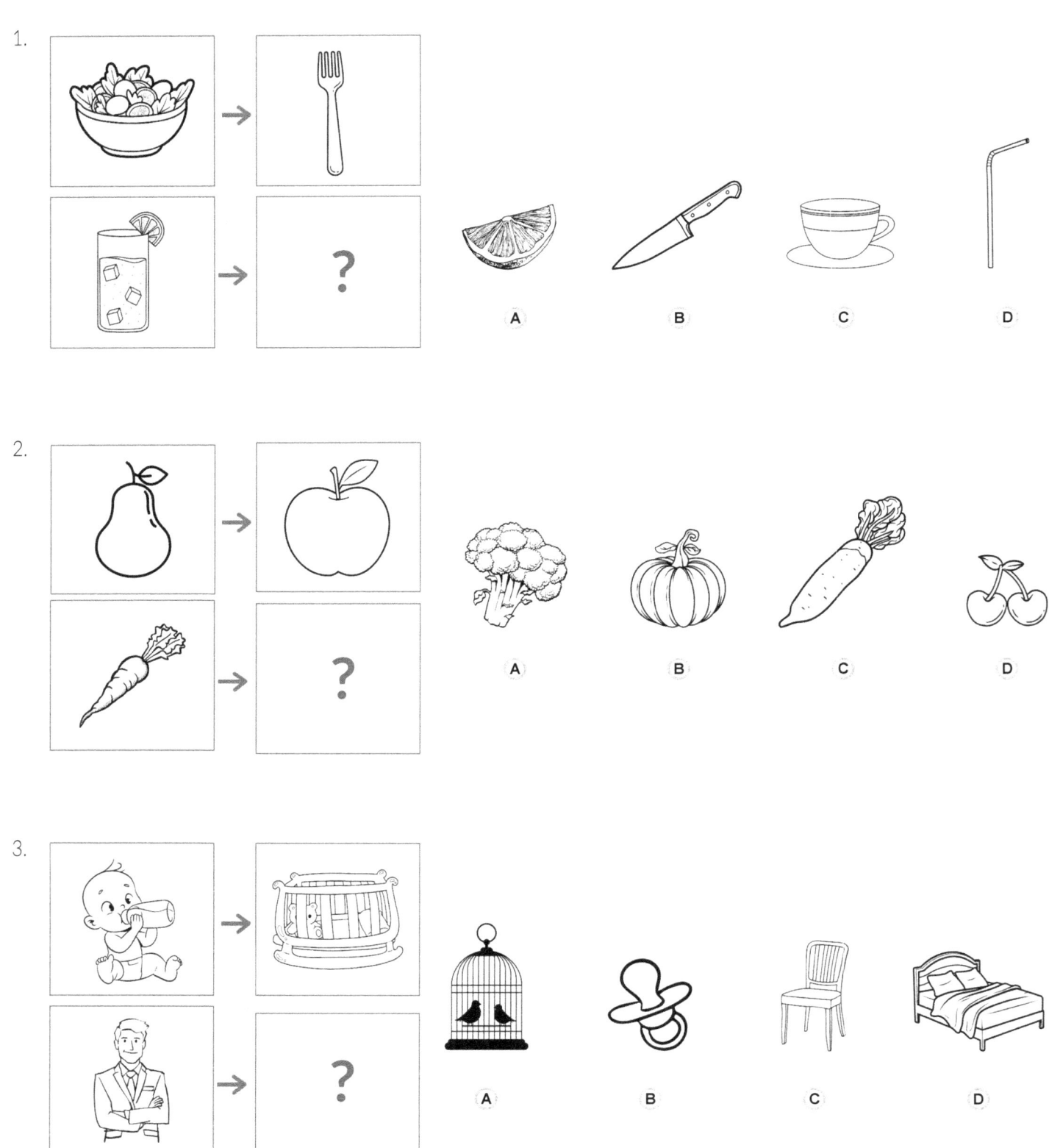

4.

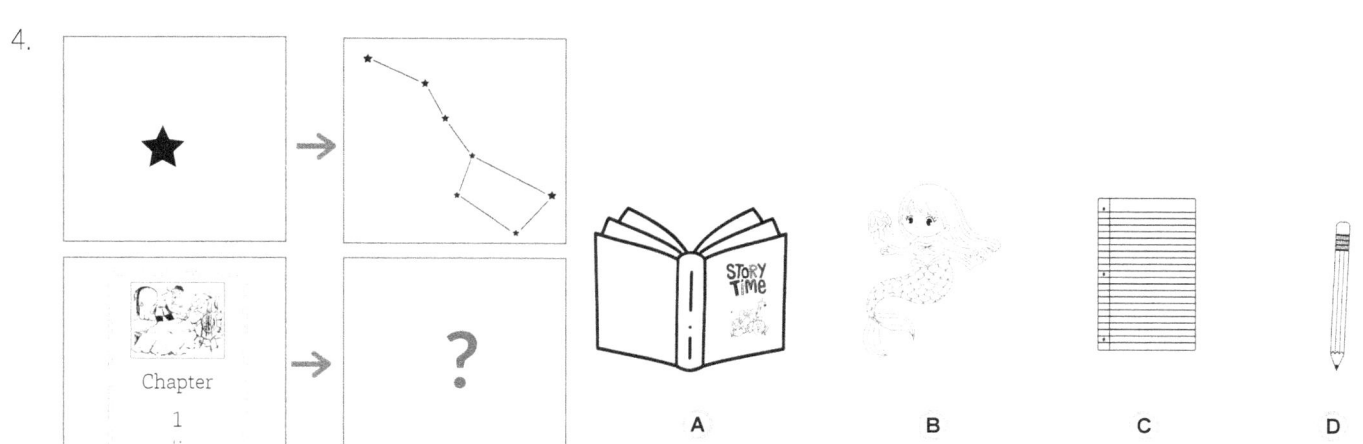

A	B	C	D

5.

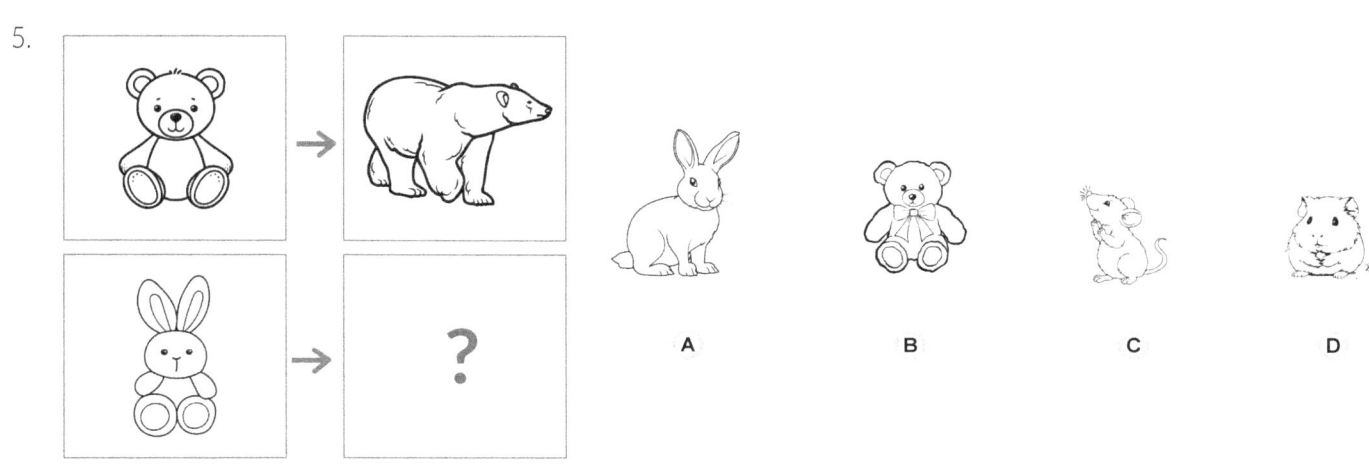

A	B	C	D

6.

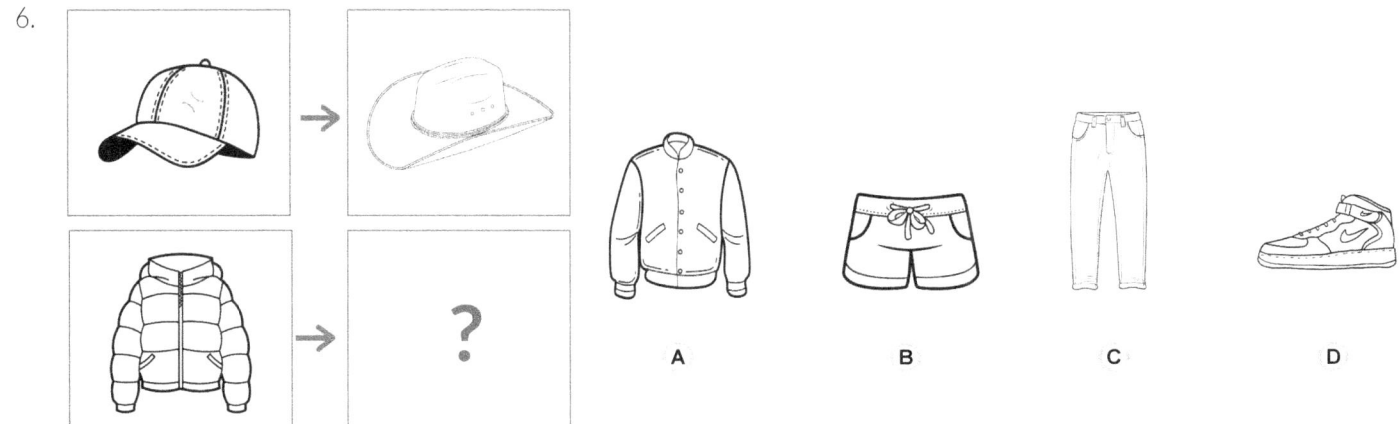

A	B	C	D

7.

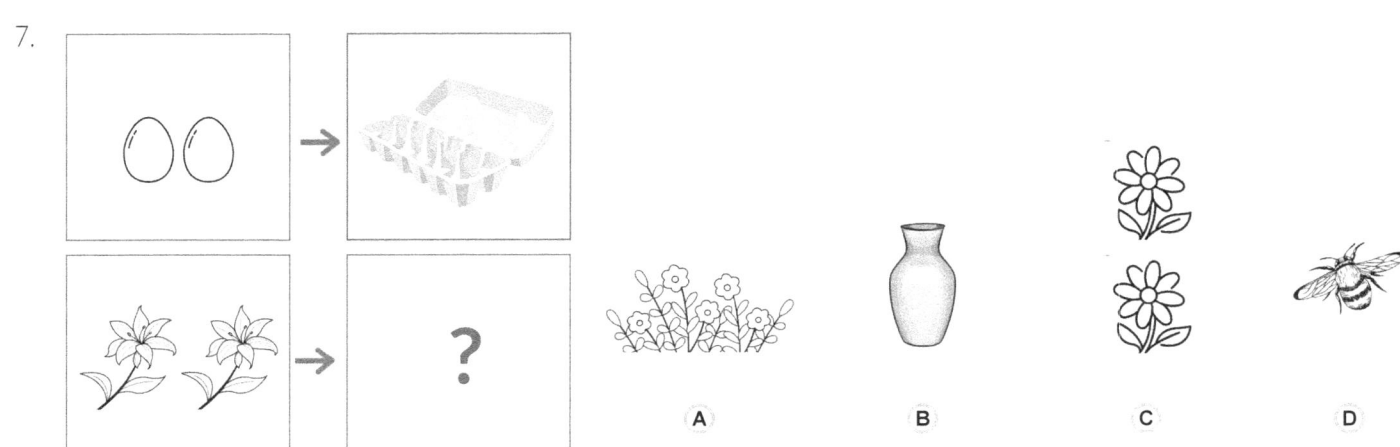

A B C D

8.

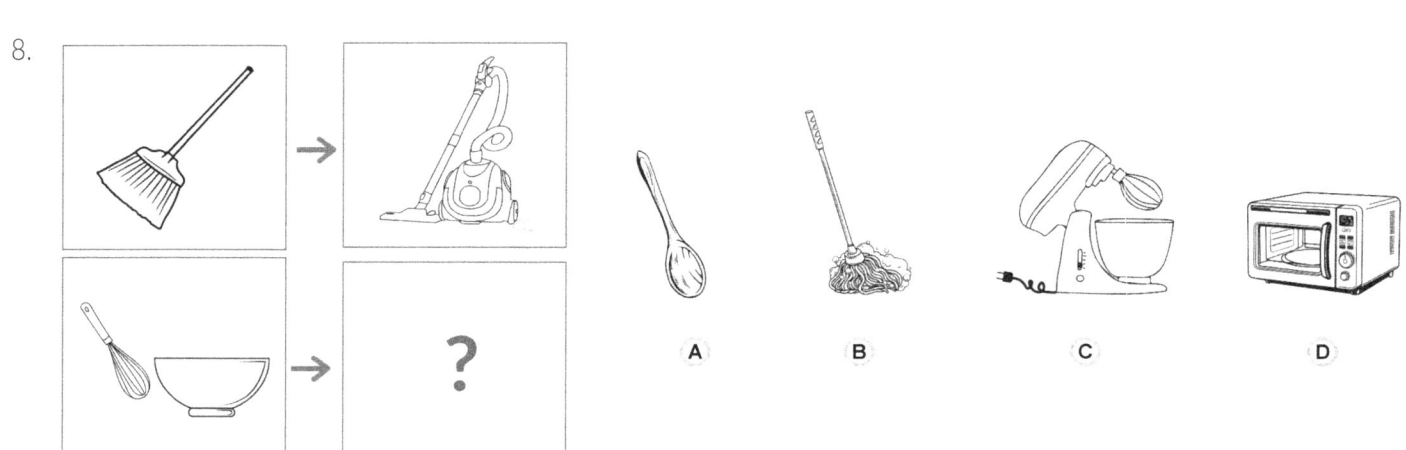

A B C D

9.

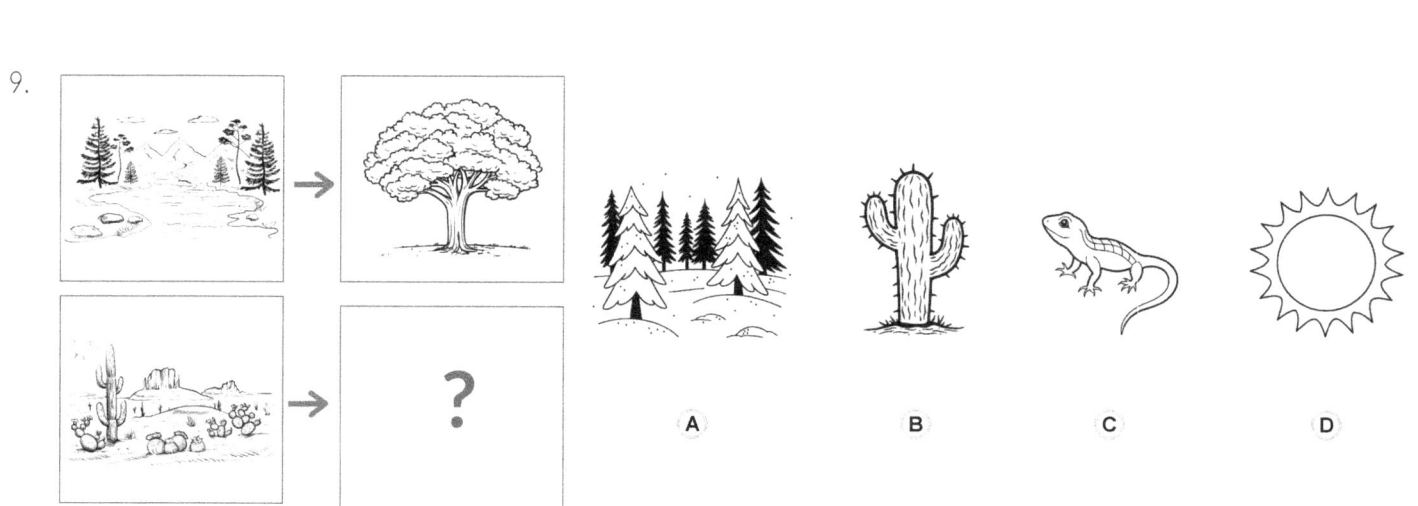

A B C D

10.

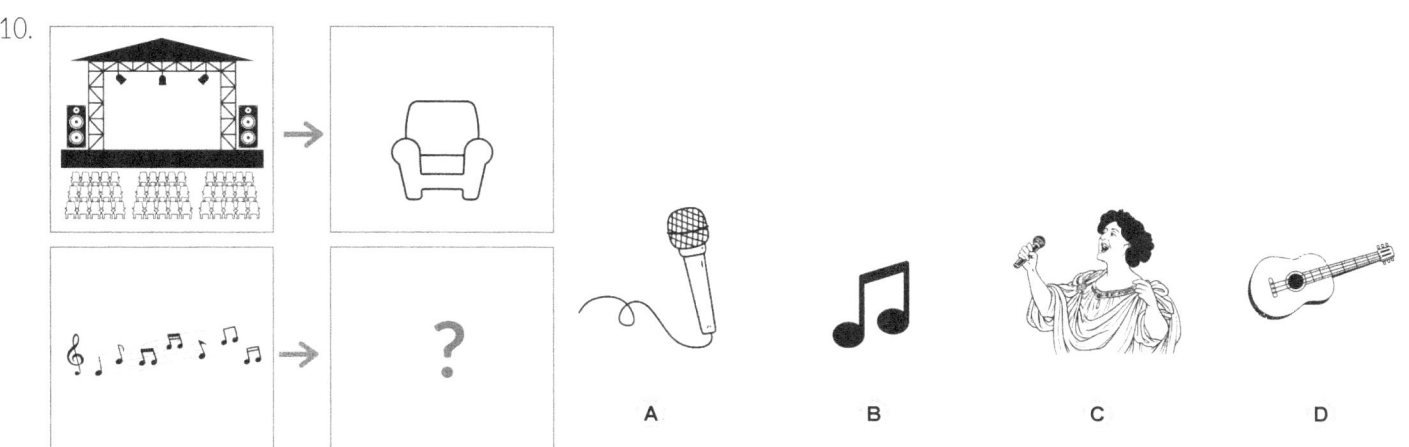

A   B   C   D

11.

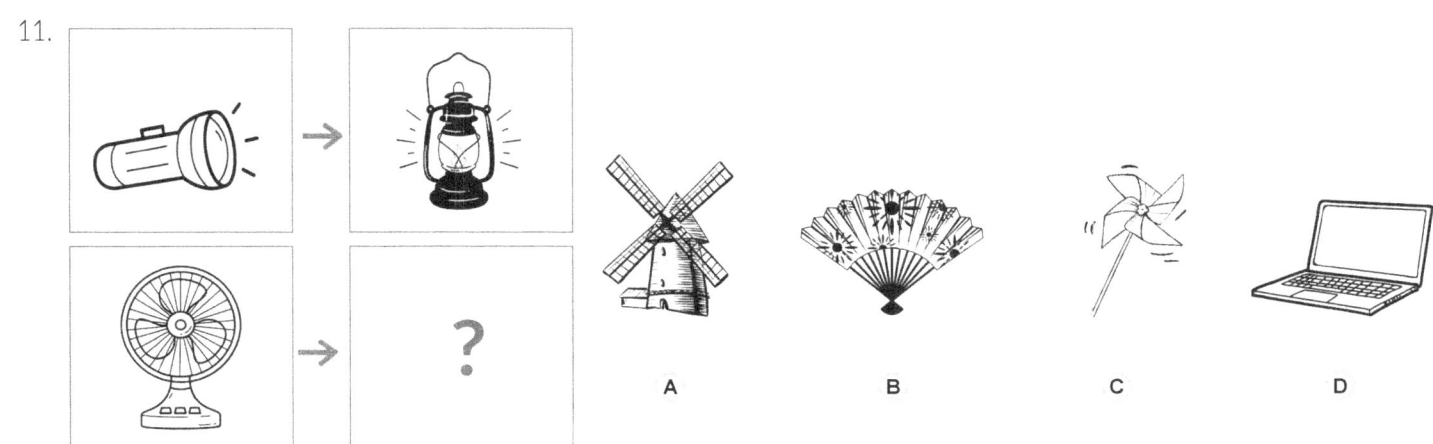

A   B   C   D

12.

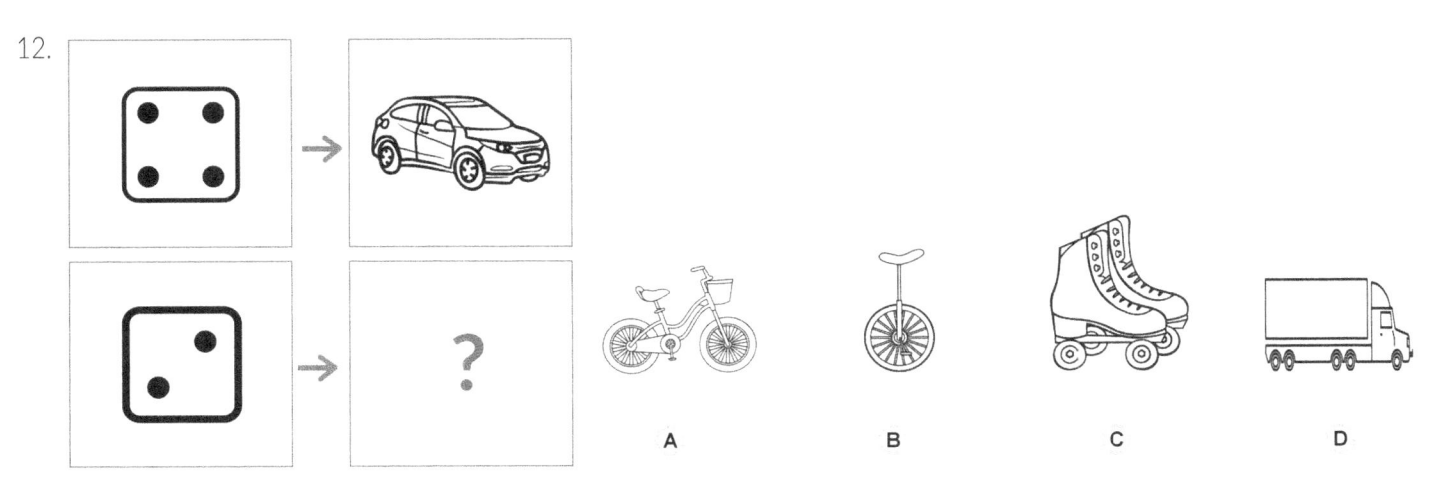

A   B   C   D

13

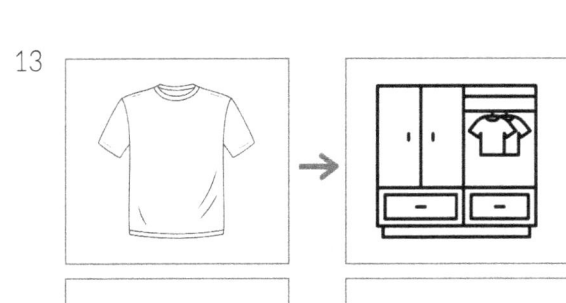

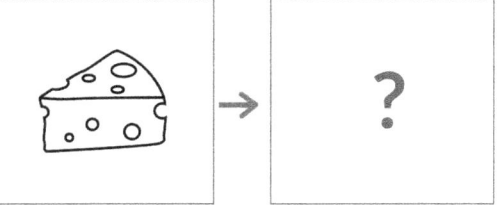

 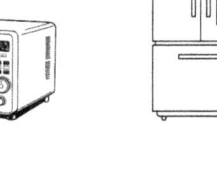 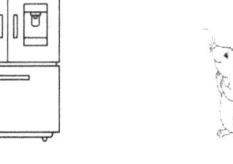 

A   B   C   D

14.

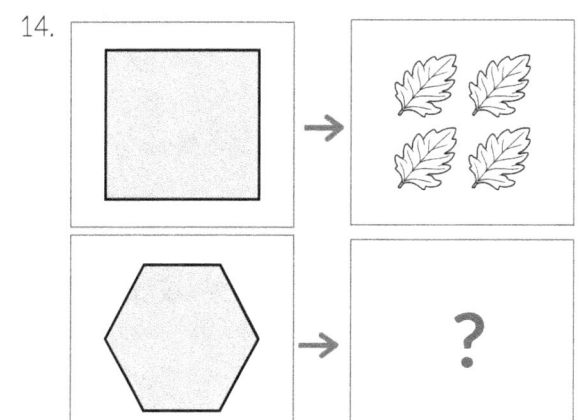

A   B   C   D

15.

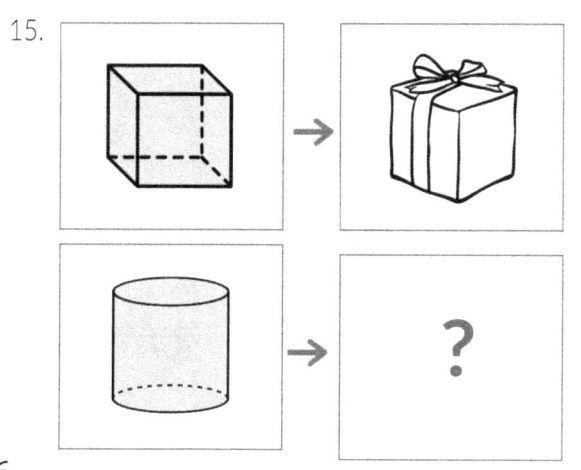

 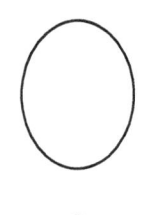  

A   B   C   D

16.

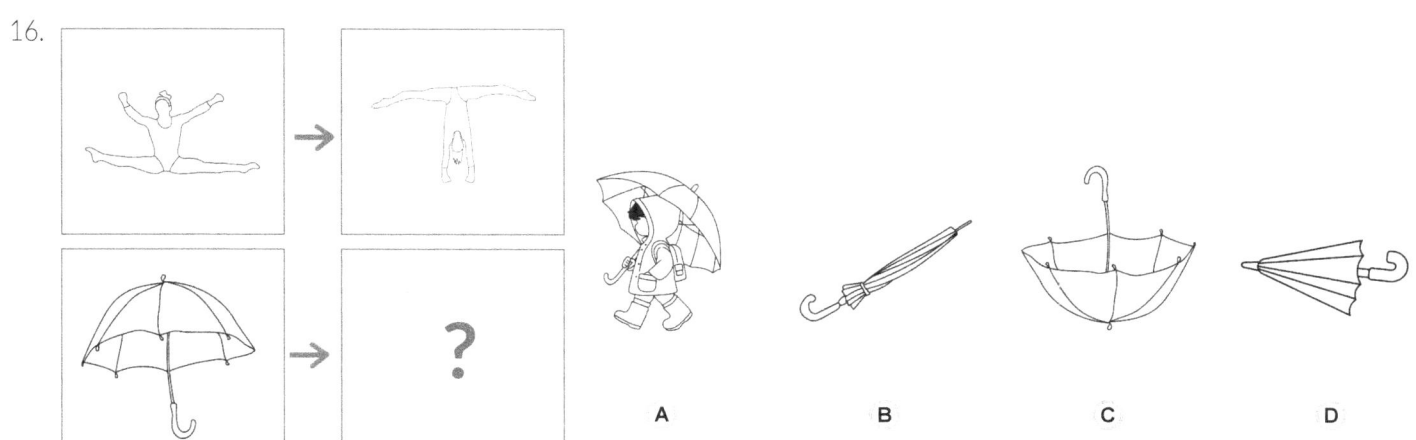

A   B   C   D

17.

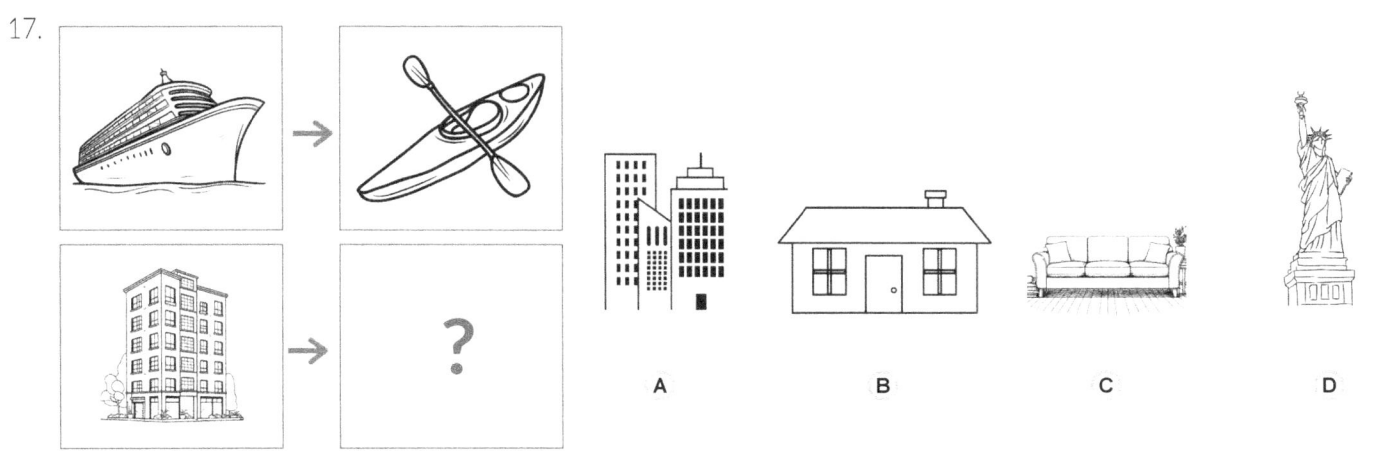

A   B   C   D

Nice Work!

Daniel

PICTURE CLASSIFICATION
Directions: The top row shows three pictures that are alike in some way. Look at the bottom row. Which bottom picture goes best with the top pictures?

1.

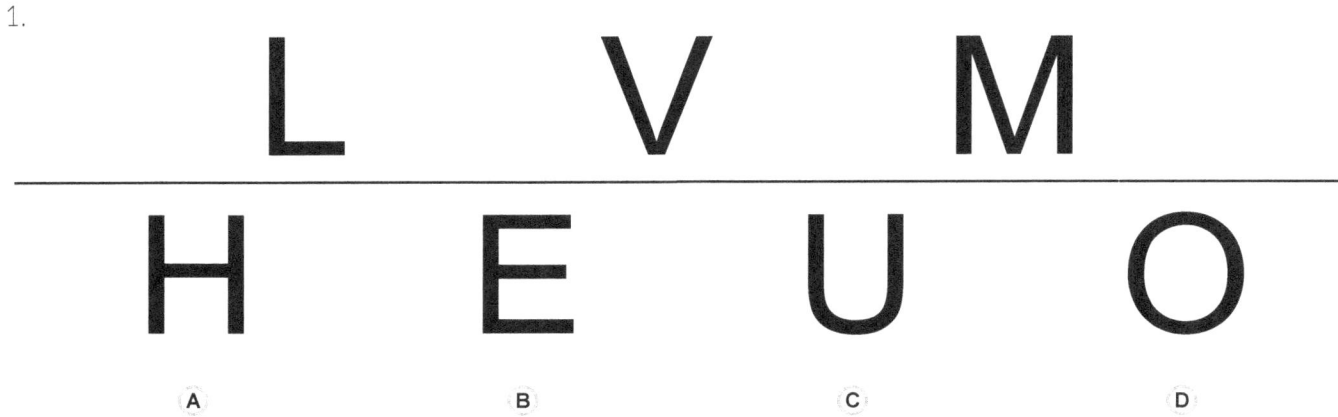

L V M

H E U O

A B C D

2.

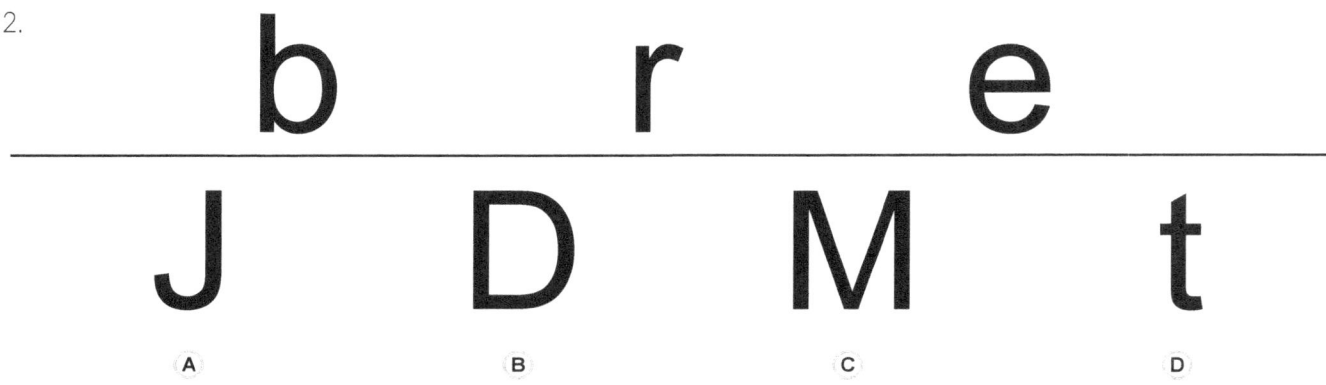

b r e

J D M t

A B C D

3.

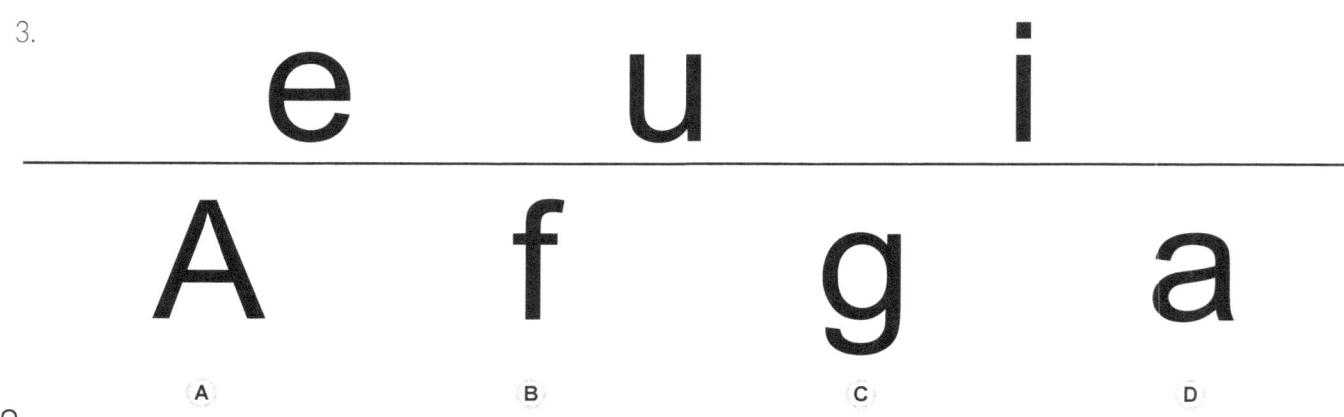

e u i

A f g a

A B C D

4.

 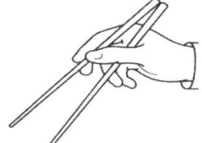 

A B C D

5.

A B C D

6.

A B C D

7.

A	B	C	D

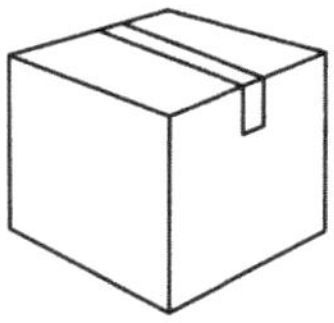

8.

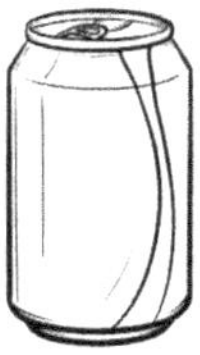

A	B	C	D

NEWS

SARDINES

9.

A	B	C	D

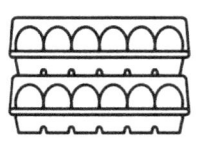

10.

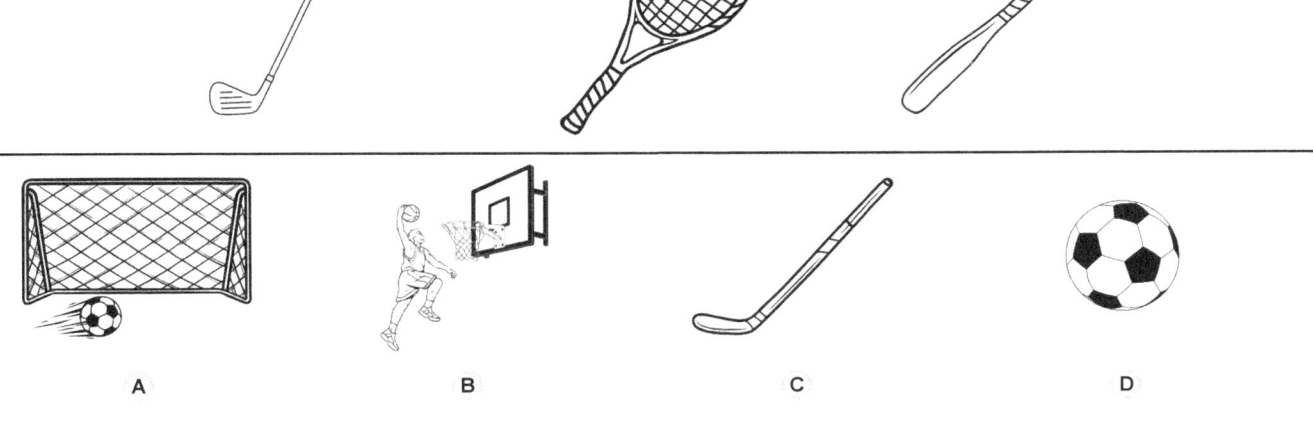

A 　　　　　　　B 　　　　　　　C 　　　　　　　D

11.

A　　　　　　　B　　　　　　　C　　　　　　　D

12.

A 　　　　　　　B 　　　　　　　C 　　　　　　　D

13.

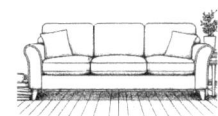 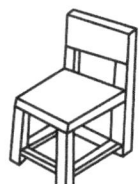 

 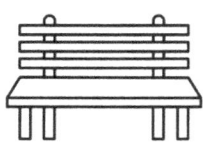  

A B C D

14.

A B C D

15.

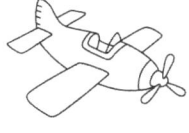   

A B C D

16.

A   **B**   **C**   **D**

17.

A   **B**   **C**   **D**

18.

  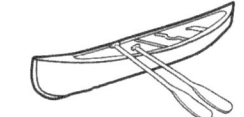

   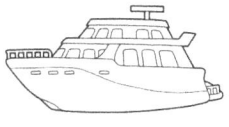

A   **B**   **C**   **D**

SENTENCE COMPLETION

Directions: Listen to the question, then choose the best answer.

1. If you wanted to cook pasta, which one would you use?

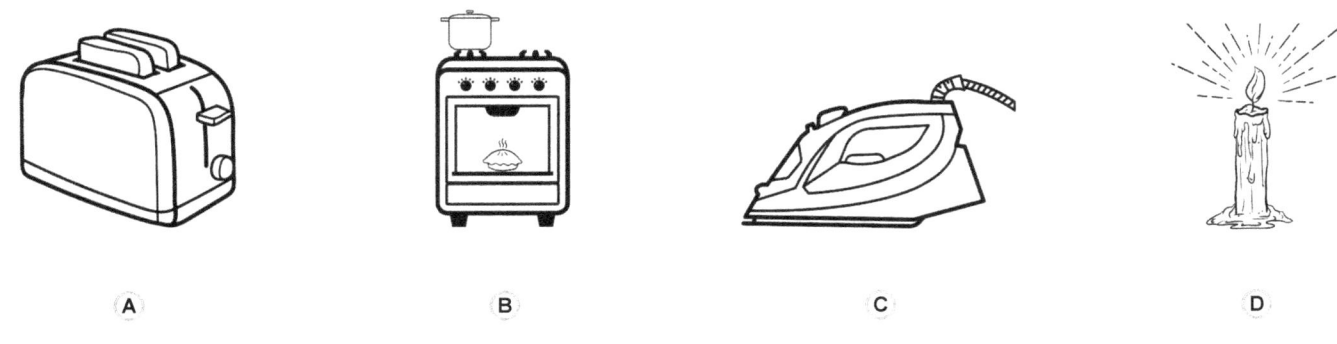

| A | B | C | D |

2. Which one of these would travel across a large lake the fastest?

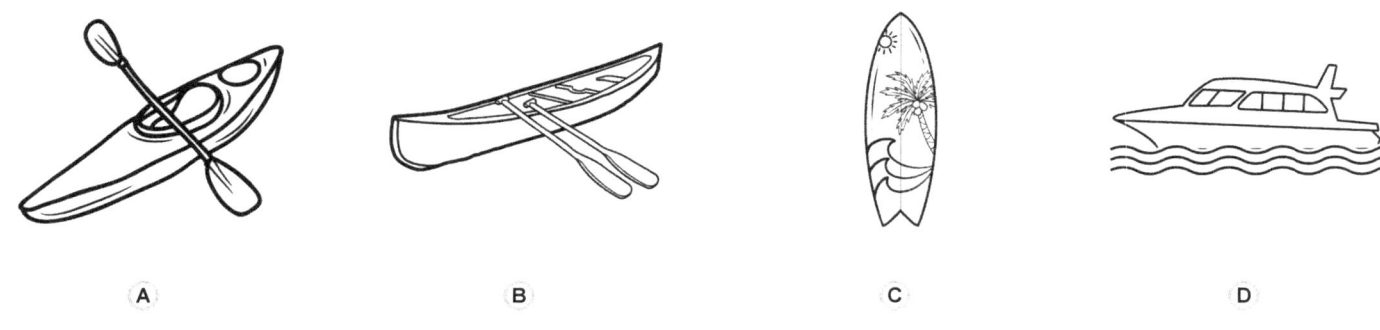

| A | B | C | D |

3. If you needed to weigh something, which one would be the best to use?

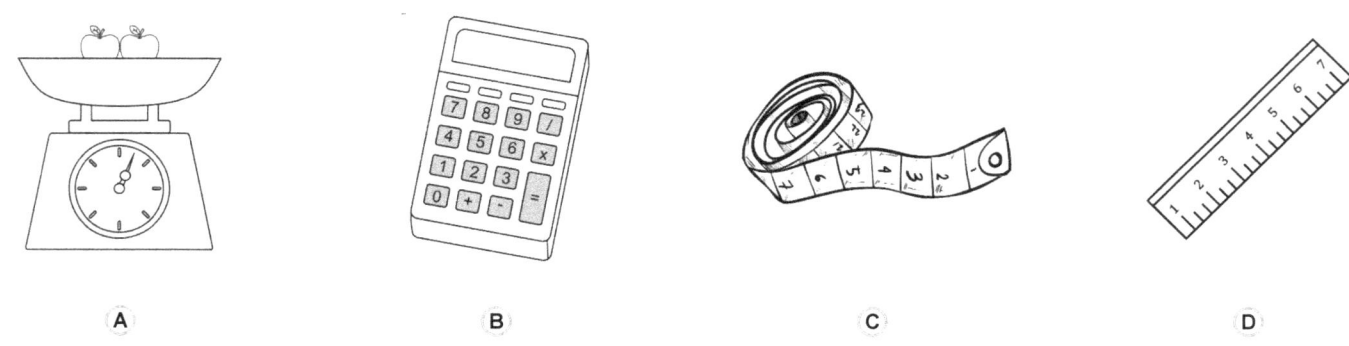

| A | B | C | D |

4. Which shows a circle in the middle, with a star on the top and a square on the bottom?

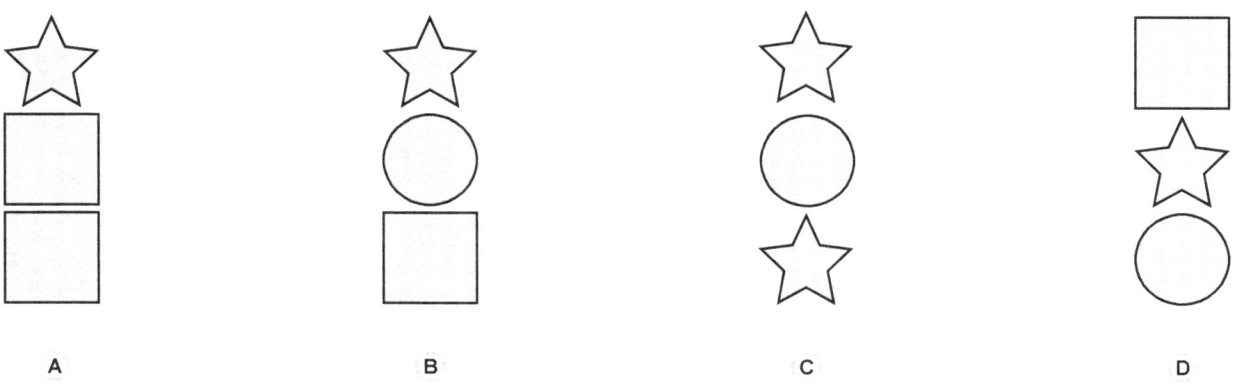

A   B   C   D

5. If the electricity went out where you live, which one of these would still work?

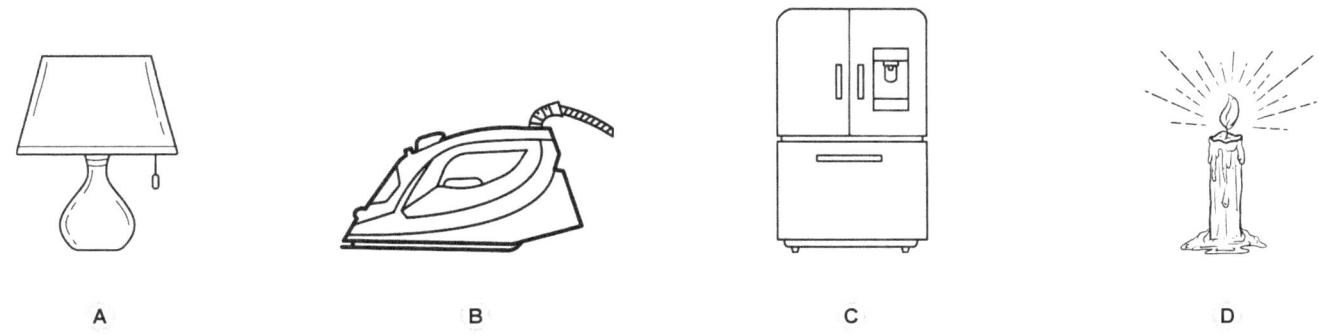

A   B   C   D

6. Which choice shows two shapes that are both 3-D shapes?

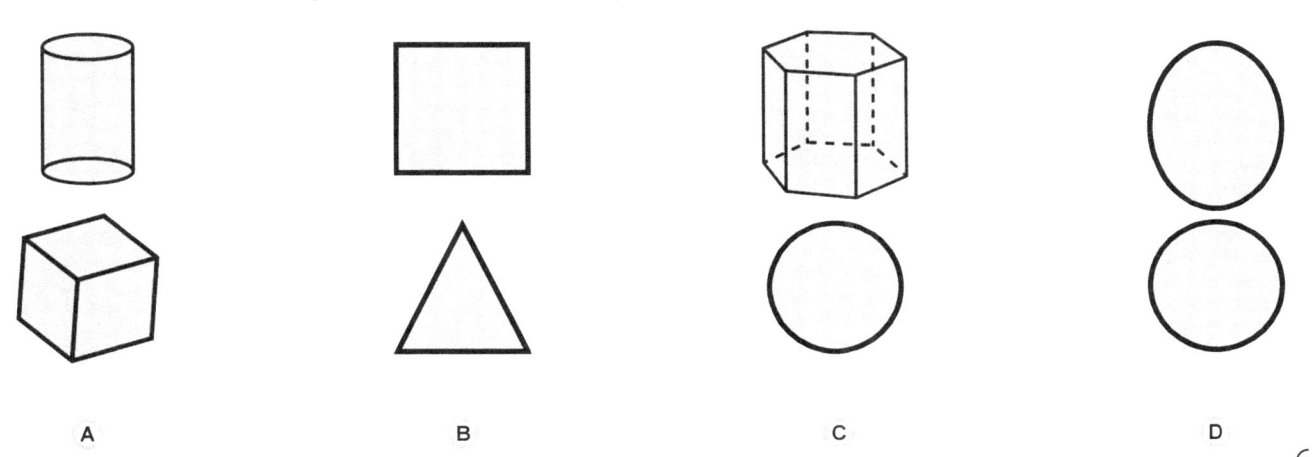

A   B   C   D

7. Which picture shows 2 objects that are used for measuring?

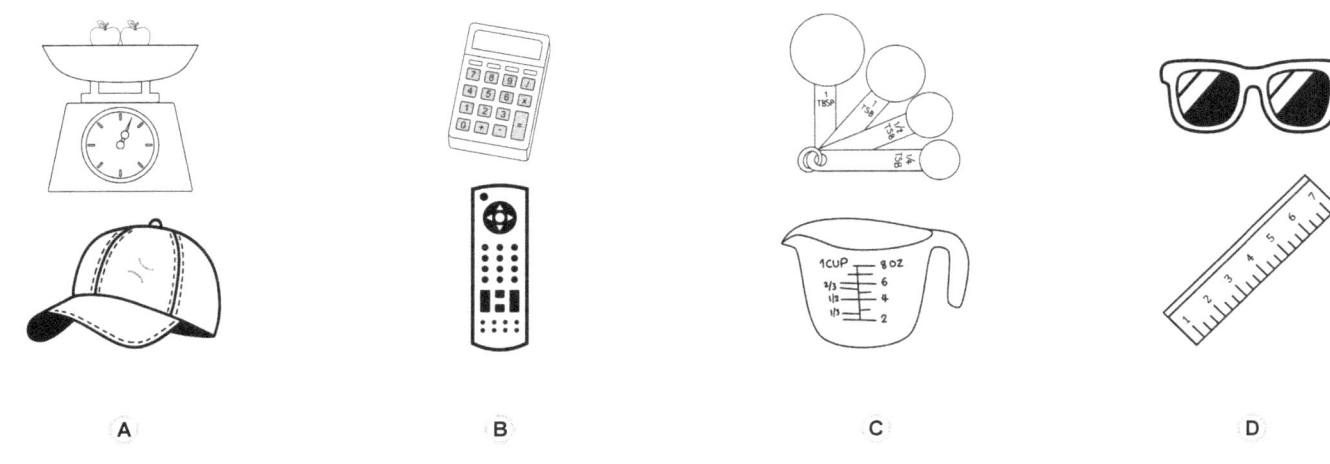

A   B   C   D

8. There are three things in your bag: a water bottle, a book, and a pair of gloves. Which picture shows something that is not in your bag?

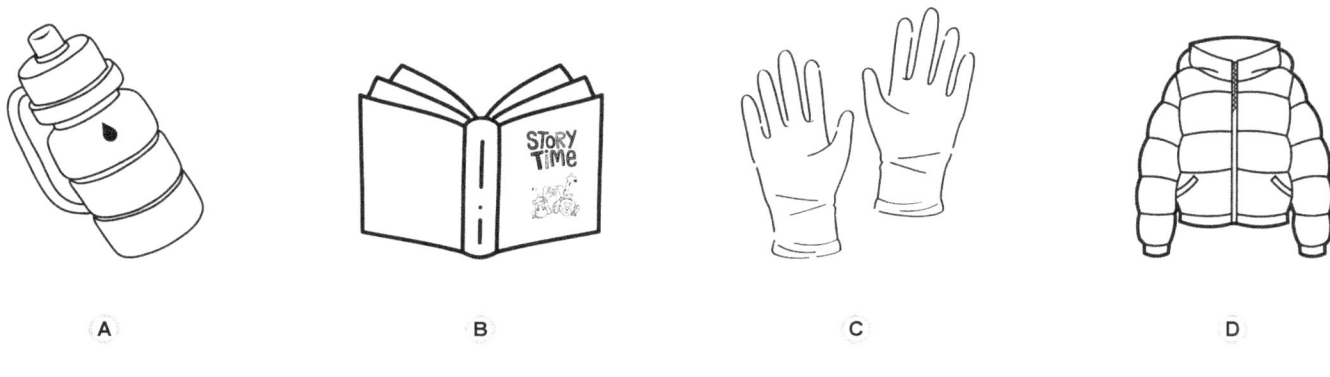

A   B   C   D

9. You read a book about two animals. One animal lives in the desert, and the other lives in the rainforest. Which picture shows the animals from your book?

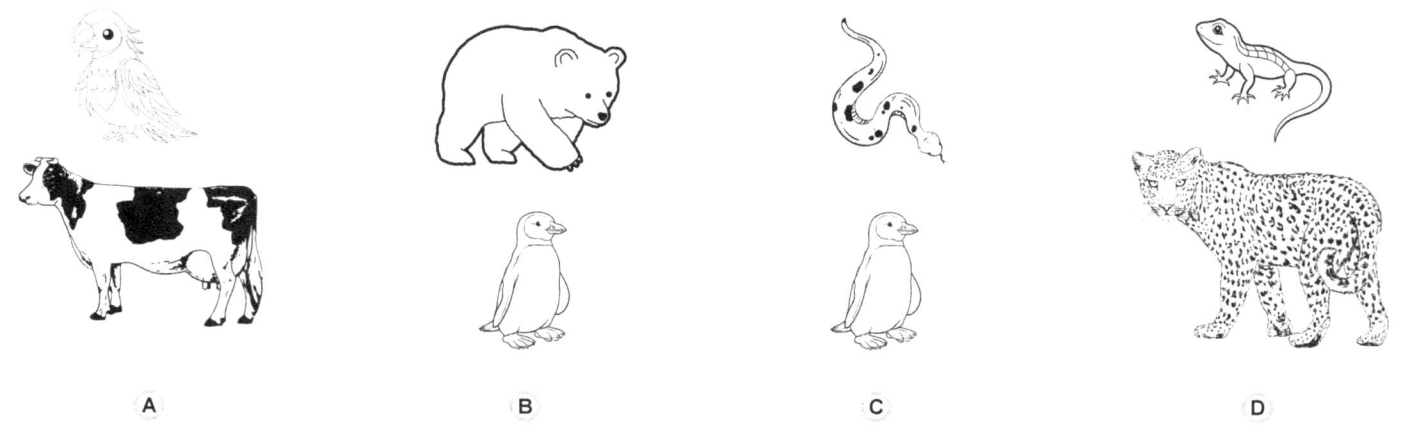

A   B   C   D

10. Which one shows something that is not used to measure height?

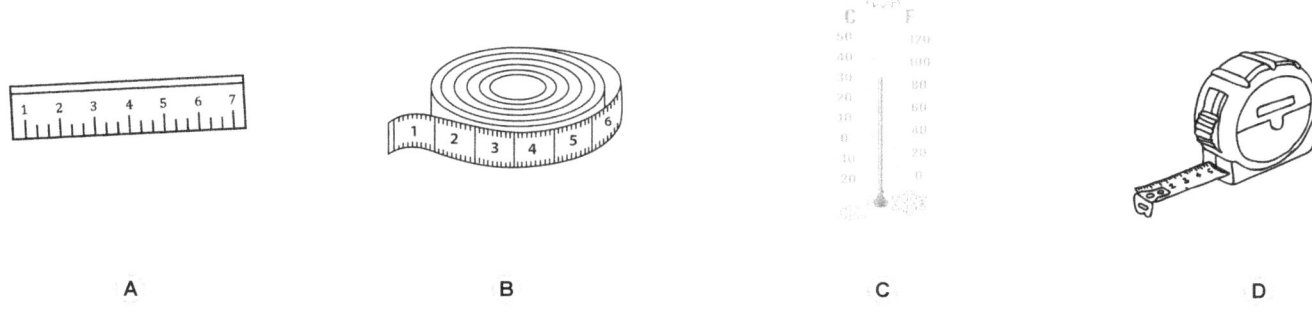

A　　　　　　　　B　　　　　　　　C　　　　　　　　D

11. In which of the places below would you see an iceberg?

A　　　　　　　　B　　　　　　　　C　　　　　　　　D

12. Which picture shows something designed by an architect?

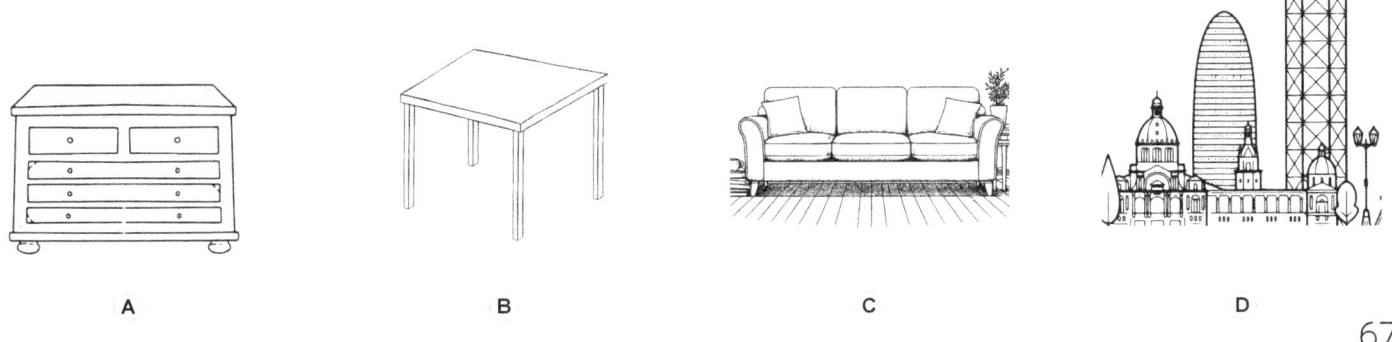

A　　　　　　　　B　　　　　　　　C　　　　　　　　D

13. Which group of animals has the most mammals?

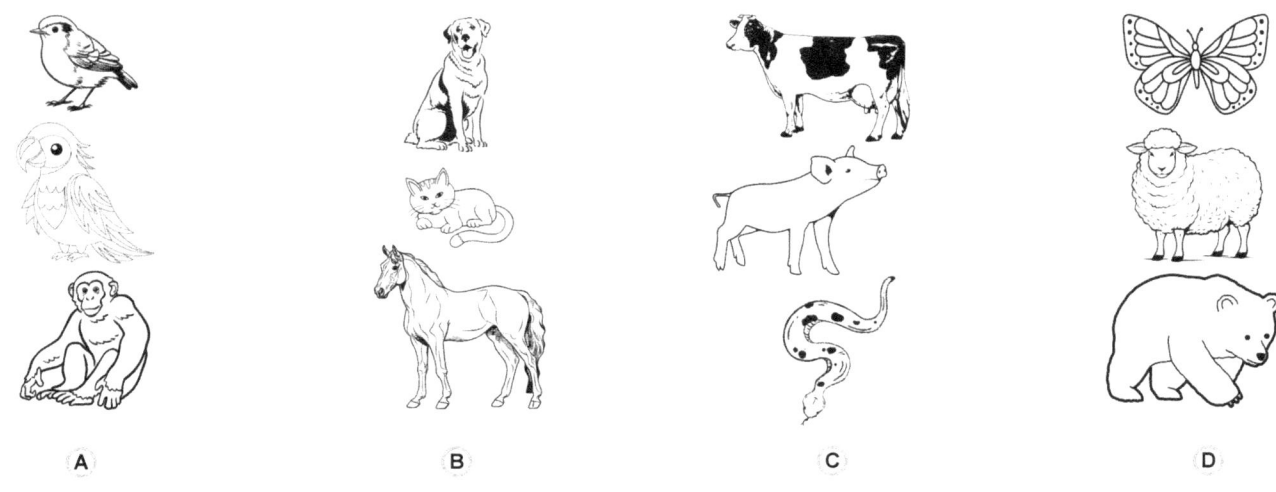

A   B   C   D

14. Which animal below would travel the slowest?

A 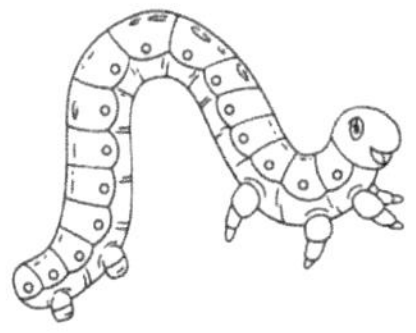   B    C    D

Excellent job! You answered all the questions!

Ana   Neil

ANSWER KEYS

ANSWER KEY FOR PRACTICE TEST 1

Picture Analogies, Practice Test 1

1. C. A saw is used to cut a tree, as a kitchen knife is used with an apple.

2. C. A watch and stopwatch are used to tell time, as glasses and a magnifying glass are used to see things up close. (Also, the first objects, a watch and glasses, are worn on the body. The second objects are held in your hand.)

3. D. An open version of the object appears on the left, while a closed version of the object appears on the right.

4. B. The objects have similar functions. A sock and skate are worn on the feet. A helmet and crown are worn on the head.

5. A. One egg and then a group of eggs in a container; one flower and then a group of flowers in a container.

6. D. The object on the left shows the time of day/night that the bird on the right is active. During the day, a hawk is active and looking for prey. During the night, an owl is active and looking for prey.

7. A. The object on the left shows a pretend version of a related animal on the right. A dragon is a pretend reptile, while a lizard is a real reptile. A unicorn is the pretend version of a horse.

8. D. Opposites. On and off on top. Unlocked and locked on the bottom.

9. D. On the left is the adult male version (man/rooster) of the baby/chick.

10. A. The number of circles on the left is the same as the number of sides that the shape on the right has.

11. B. A half version appears on the left. A whole version appears on the right.

12. A. On the left the object(s) are open, while on the right the objects are closed.

13. C. On the left is the animal that lives in the man-made home on the right.

14. C. On the left is a motorized version of the object on the right.

15. A. The number of dots on the dice is the same number of legs that the animal on the right has.

16. B. On the right is an animal that makes/helps make the food on the left.

17. B. On the left is the old-fashioned version of the new, modern version of the object on the right.

18. D. The object on the left (bread/paper) comes from the object on the right (wheat/a tree).

Picture Classification, Practice Test 1

1. D. instruments

2. D. vehicles that travel in the air

3. D. vegetables

4. B. insects

5. D. spherical objects (objects shaped like spheres)

Picture Classification, Practice Test 1, continued

6. C. different kinds of shells
7. B. objects that hold things together
8. D. closed objects
9. B. dairy products
10. C. vowels
11. C. halves
12. B. things that grow on trees
13. A. the objects have spots
14. D. pre-historic animals
15. C. things made out of wood
16. C. objects used to tell time
17. D. objects used for measuring
18. C. different kinds of feet

Sentence Completion, Practice Test 1

1. D. A fireman puts out fires.
2. B. A bear hibernates.
3. C. Dental floss is used to clean in between teeth.
4. A. A violinist plays a violin.
5. C. A strawberry has the most seeds.
6. A. A whisk is used to mix ingredients for baked goods.
7. B. A pair of scissors cuts, a crayon colors, and a ruler measures.
8. D. A scene with smoke coming out of the chimney and snowy mountains shows us that the weather is cold.
9. C. Water would no longer be able to fill the bathtub.
10. B. A snake does not have legs.
11. A. A dinosaur is a prehistoric animal.
12. C. The ocean animals are a dolphin, lobster, and fish. A cow lives on land.
13. B. This is a tropical place, as indicated by the plants and animals shown.
14. D. The fast train is the only modern thing shown.
15. C. Cherries grow on trees.
16. D. A popsicle is frozen.

ANSWER KEY FOR PRACTICE TEST 2

Picture Analogies, Practice Test 2

1. D. The food on the left is commonly eaten by the animal on the right.
2. B. The tool on the left is used by the worker on the right (a fireman/a farmer).
3. A. The object on the left is the home of the animal on the right.
4. B. The number on the left equals the number of sides of the shape on the right.
5. A. The worker on the left makes the item on the right.
6. A. Objects with similar functions are in the left and right boxes. Measuring objects are on top. Objects used to make things appear larger (glasses and a microscope) are on the bottom.
7. B. Similar drinks/foods are in the left and right boxes. On top, juice and coffee/tea are both liquids. On the bottom, an apple and cherries are both fruit that grow on trees.
8. B. The body parts on the left are covered by the accessory on the right.
9. C. The object on the left (a pan lid/blanket) covers the object on the right (a pan/a bed).
10. A. The body part on the left is used with the object on the right. You use your mouth with a whistle. You use your eye with a microscope.
11. B. The object on the left is made out of the object on the right. A log cabin is made from logs. A sweater is made from yarn.
12. D. The objects have similar functions. On top, the objects hold paper together. On the bottom, the objects are used for measurement.
13. B. On the left is the side view. On the right in the front view of the same thing.
14. B. Similar animals are in the left and right boxes. Reptiles are on top. Birds are on the bottom.
15. B. On the left is the animal. On the right is the animal's habitat.
16. C. On the left is the food used to make the food product on the right.
17. D. On the left is a non-electric/non-motorized version of the object on the right.
18. A. On the left is a non-electric/non-motorized version of the object on the right.

Picture Classification, Practice Test 2

1. A. sea animals
2. D. farm animals that are mammals
3. C. objects used to carry things
4. A. objects found in kitchens
5. D. animal homes
6. B. hot objects
7. D. things having to do with "4": 4 identical puppies, a four-sided shape, a dice with 4 dots, a 4-leaf clover
8. C. things that come in pairs

9. D. things used for cutting
10. B. open objects
11. D. birds
12. C. things that are used for light
13. A. kinds of homes
14. C. tools
15. A. clothing worn on lower half of body
16. A. things that have holes
17. D. things worn on upper half of body
18. C. things having to do with "3": a tricycle, three pigs, a triangle, a stoplight with 3 lights

Sentence Completion, Practice Test 2

1. A. The pair of shorts is the only warm weather clothing.
2. C. You wouldn't find an iron in a classroom.
3. D. Dice come in pairs.
4. B. This is a container used for measuring.
5. A. A stove and a pan are used for cooking.
6. B. This choice shows the 2 shapes: a circle for an apple and a triangle for a banana.
7. C. Bread is not a plant, and it does not come from an animal.
8. C. An octopus lives underwater, and a squirrel can climb trees.
9. A. A polar bear and a penguin only live in cold climates.
10. D. The pyramids (of Egypt) are ancient. The others are modern.
11. A. Cheese comes from an animal, as milk comes from cows.
12. B. Sheep live in herds.
13. C. Rain is a form of precipitation. If it rains, you would need an umbrella.
14. A. You can put items in a safe.
15. D. A pear is a food picked from a tree. Grapes grow on a vine.
16. D. You would not see a microscope at a construction site.

ANSWER KEY FOR PRACTICE TEST 3

Picture Analogies, Practice Test 3

1. D. On the left is the food/drink. On the right is the object used to consume it.
2. C. Similar foods on the left and right. On top, both are fruit grown on trees. On the bottom, both are vegetables grown under the ground/root vegetables.
3. D. On the left is the baby/man. On the right is where they sleep (a crib/bed).
4. A. The object on the left (a star, a book's page) makes up the object on the right (a constellation, a book).
5. A. On the left is a toy version of the animal on the right.
6. A. Similar objects on the left and right. On top are hats. On the bottom are jackets.
7. B. The objects on the left (eggs, flowers) go together and are stored in the object on the right (egg carton, vase).
8. C. The object on the left is a slower, non-motorized version (a broom/whisk and bowl) of the object on the right (a vacuum and mixer).
9. B. The place on the left is the habitat of the plant on the right.
10. B. On the left is a grouped version (a theatre with many seats, a group of music notes) of the object on the right (a seat, music note).
11. B. On the left is a powered version (a flashlight, fan) of the object on the right (a lantern, a hand-held fan).
12. A. The number of dots on the dice equals the number of vehicle wheels.
13. B. The object on the left is stored in the object on the right.
14. A. The number of shape sides equals the number of objects on the right.
15. D. The object on the left and right have the same 3-D shape (cube and cylinder).
16. C. The object on the right is an upside-down version of the object on the left.
17. B. The object on the left holds many people inside. The object on the right is a version of this that only holds one or a few people. On top, the objects are vehicles for traveling on the water. On the bottom, the objects are places people live (or work).

Picture Classification, Practice Test 3

1. A. consonants
2. D. lower case letters
3. D. lower case vowels
4. D. things that come in pairs
5. D. things that hold liquids
6. C. things that have stripes
7. C. cube-shaped objects
8. A. cylinder-shaped objects

Picture Classification, Practice Test 3, continued

9. C. things that come in a group
10. A. vehicles with motors/engines
11. C. sports equipment used for hitting
12. A. real vehicles (the others are toys)
13. B. objects used for sitting
14. D. objects that have wheels
15. C. vehicles that carry many people
16. D. adult versions of animals (the others are babies or a tadpole)
17. A. insects
18. C. vehicles without motors

Sentence Completion, Practice Test 3

1. B. You would use a stove to cook pasta.
2. D. A boat with a motor would go the fastest.
3. A. A scale weighs items.
4. B.
5. D. A candle would still work as it does not use electricity.
6. A. A cylinder and a cube are both 3-D shapes.
7. C. Measuring spoons and a measuring cup are both used for measuring.
8. D. A jacket is not in the bag.
9. D. A lizard lives in the desert. A jaguar lives in the rainforest.
10. C. A thermometer is not used to measure height. It measures temperature.
11. B. You would see an iceberg in very cold areas, like choice B. (The other choices show warm weather.)
12. D. Choice D shows buildings, which architects design. (The other choices show furniture, which architects do not design.)
13. B. All the animals shown are mammals.
14. B. A worm travels the slowest.

Need more practice?

- Help your child **ace the test**!

- Check out **Savant Test Prep**™ books on Amazon®.